THE VALUE OF ASSOCIATIONS TO AMERICAN SOCIETY

A Report by the Hudson Institute

Published by the
American Society of Association Executives
and
The Foundation of the American Society of Association Executives

Cover design, typographic design,
and composition: Design Consultants, Inc.
Falls Church, Virginia
Editor: Heidi H. Bowers, ASAE, Washington, D.C.
Proofreading: Editorial Experts, Inc.
Alexandria, Virginia
Printing: United Book Press
Baltimore, Maryland

ISBN 0-88034-041-X

American Society of Association Executives
1575 Eye Street, N.W.
Washington, D.C. 20005-1168

Printed in the United States of America

★ ★ ★ ★ Contents

★ ★ ★ ★ Foreword

It is no secret that associations have a profound impact on American society. But, even though associations are intimately woven into the fabric of American life, until now little has been known about the breadth and depth of their contributions. What most Americans know about the unique roles of associations in our nation has been limited to their personal experience. It's almost as if associations as a whole are an invisible part of the private and government sectors.

We turned to the Hudson Institute, a prestigious think tank known for its objectivity, to ask that it accept the challenge of measuring the value of associations to America in both economic and noneconomic terms.

Mark Blitz, the study team leader and chief author of the book, indicates that the numbers reported for the economic value assigned to association activities, while impressive, are very conservative. They represent *only* those 5,500 associations identified as part of the survey. It is this kind of devotion to absolute credibility that makes the survey results reliable and believable. Blitz's commentary on the social value of associations as providers of education, producers of standards and codes of ethics, and participants in the political process concludes that *Associations Advance America*.

Your comments are always welcome.

R. William Taylor, CAE
President
American Society of Association Executives
Washington, D.C.
July 1990

 # Acknowledgments

The members and staff of the American Society of Association Executives are grateful to the many individuals who participated in the design and review of this book. Their tenacious efforts have made this a noteworthy dissertation on the value of associations.

Members of The Hudson Institute Study Task Force include Chairman Donald G. Weinert, PE, CAE, National Society of Professional Engineers, Alexandria, Virginia; Robert S. Bolan, CAE, American Diabetes Association, Alexandria, Virginia; Anne L. Bryant, Ed.D., CAE, American Association of University Women, Washington, D.C.; William D. Coughlan, CAE, American Physical Therapy Association, Alexandria, Virginia; John B. Cox, CAE, National Association of College and University Business Officers, Washington, D.C.; and Gene N. Fondren, CAE, Texas Automobile Dealers Association, Austin. Also, Donald K. Gardiner, CAE, National Association of Professional Insurance Agents, Alexandria, Virginia; Kenneth F. Hine, CAE, American Hotel and Motel Association, Washington, D.C.; Kathryn E. Johnson, CAE, The Healthcare Forum, San Francisco; Paul T. Knapp, CAE, American Institute of Architects, Washington, D.C.; Dadie Perlov, CAE, The Consensus Management Group, New York; Almon R. Smith, Ph.D., CAE, Ohio Association of Realtors, Columbus; and R. William Taylor, CAE, American Society of Association Executives, Washington, D.C.

The study was conducted and written principally by Mark Blitz, Ph.D., director of political and social studies, with contributions from David Reed, DBA, chief domestic economist, and David Weinschrott, Ph.D., research fellow, all of the Hudson Institute, Indianapolis.

Special thanks is due to the members of the special ad hoc task force on the Hudson Institute study of ASAE's 1989–1990 Communication Section Council for their dedicated work in developing the structure of the communication plan used to disseminate the information in this report.

Also assisting ASAE in developing communication plans were Elizabeth J. Allen, CAE, International Association of Business Communicators, San Francisco; Catherine D. Bower, CAE, Society for Human Resource Management, Alexandria, Virginia; George D. Kirkland, CAE, Los Angeles Convention and Visitors Bureau; Elizabeth A. Kovacs, CAE, Public Relations Society of America, New York; J. C. Mahaffey, CAE, Chicago Society of Association Executives; and several members of the Hudson Institute Study Task Force.

Heidi H. Bowers, ASAE book editor, added significantly to the value of the book. ASAE staff Thomas A. Gorski, director of public relations and market research, and Elissa M. Myers, CAE, director of publishing, also made important contributions adding to the integrity of this publication.

 # Exploring Associations' Value

KEY FINDINGS

- ☐ Associations allow "goods" such as knowledge and friendship to be produced and enhanced among like-minded people.
- ☐ Associations offer a collective presence as producers and providers to the collective presence of buyers.
- ☐ Associations' central functions are not arbitrary but arise to enhance pursuit of collective interests.
- ☐ The public value of associations is largely a consequence of their intelligent pursuit of collective interest.

"Associations exist first to serve those member interests not met sufficiently through individual action."

The importance and value of associations has been noticed by every observer of American life at least since Alexis de Tocqueville, the nineteenth-century French statesman and author. Associations, indeed, are one element distinguishing America from other countries. In no other nation are associations as independent or as pervasive, yet, the worth of associations is often seen only in terms of what they do for their members and for the general spirit of limited, responsible government. This book attempts to reach beyond that view by exploring specific areas of public value that associations generate.

The study hinges on discussion of two fundamental questions. Do associations impart economic and social value to American society? If they do, how can one understand and categorize that value? To investigate such questions, the American Society of Association Executives (ASAE), Washington, D.C., in 1989, commissioned the Hudson Institute, Indianapolis.

METHODOLOGY

The answer, forming the basis for this book, is that associations are indeed of public value—socially and economically—in a number of ways. This conclusion was derived by surveying associations, reviewing the association literature and relevant scholarly materials, holding discussions with association executives, and attending various association executives' meetings.

First, a survey was conducted of trade, professional, and cause-related and advocacy associations.[1] The survey's primary purpose was to discover the proportion of associations involved in activities offering value beyond their memberships. A secondary purpose was to uncover basic economic data about association expenditures. The survey universe consisted of all associations on ASAE's list of members and prospective members,[2] and the sample was stratified to adequately represent three groups, comprising trade associations, professional associations, and cause-related and advocacy organizations.

ASAE's files of actual and prospective members represent most major trade and professional associations. The data reported reflect the universe of these groups with two caveats: (1) the limitations of survey methodology and (2) the consideration that associations estimated some expenditures not grouped in accounting terms.

Because ASAE's membership roles include a significant number of staffed cause-related and advocacy organizations but not all of them, the survey results do not fully cover these associations.[3] However, the results for cause-related and advocacy groups are still important, because the primary purpose of the survey was to uncover broad information about the extent of association activity in various areas.

The economic data generated by the survey are subject to the same caveats previously enumerated, as well as several others discussed in the economics chapter. The survey results most likely understate associations' overall economic impact.

WHY ASSOCIATIONS EXIST

Associations exist first to serve those interests of their members or their public constituencies not met sufficiently through individual action. Both associations composed of individuals and those composed of business firms serve the collective interests of their members or constituencies.

One form of this collective interest is the wish for fraternity among the like-minded or similarly employed. Hence, associations are the focus of a dizzying array of meetings and conventions. Equally important is the members' collective need to discuss what is happening in the common business, cause, or profession. Information, analysis, techniques, gossip, and common concerns all require a public forum if they are to be generated, thought through, and spread with full benefit and effect. The fraternal aspect of associations, then, almost always goes hand in hand with general communication through publications, seminars, meetings, and conventions.

The collective or public goods of friendship and knowledge are supplemented by the way in which the outside world treats the participants in a business, profession, or cause as a collectivity. A particular chemical company, for example, may not be interested in the government, but the government will be interested in it for much the same reason that it is interested in other chemical companies. An individual physician, to take another example, cannot fail to see the personal effect of a headline reporting, "Medical Rip-Off: Some Doctors Raise Bills by Misclassifying Work." People with similar jobs, professions, and interests see the utility of collectively associating to deal with an outside world which treats and affects them collectively. As a result, associations have engaged in government relations, political education, and public information from early in their history.

The collective interests of people who associate also are evident in the products and services they produce and promote that have certain common characteristics when they enter the market. There are general conditions for buying and selling automobiles and screenwriters' talents, for example. There are general conditions for "buying" and "selling" research about kidney disease or support for museums.

Associations, therefore, (1) allow "goods" such as knowledge and friendship to be produced and enhanced among like-minded people; (2) offer a unified presence to those who deal with individuals as collectivities, whether the individuals wish this or not; and (3) offer a collective presence as producers and providers to the collective presence of buyers.

It is reasonable, therefore, to think of associations' primary activities—conventions; education; research; government relations; public information; product, service, and professional standards; and codes of ethics—as stemming from these three forms of collective private interest. These central functions are not arbitrary but arise to enhance the pursuit of collective interests.

DEFINING *VALUE*

The broader public value of associations arises from *collective self-interest rightly understood*. If Alexis de Tocqueville was correct in arguing that voluntary associations in America arose more from self-interest "rightly understood" than from altruism, so, too, can one say that associations create benefits for nonmembers, or broad public value, more from collective self-interest "rightly understood" than from altruism. Intelligent and responsible collective interests are firmer grounds for public benefit than altruism alone, just as individual economic interest brings greater overall economic benefit than selflessness.

In attempting to consider the social value of associations, Hudson Institute researchers faced the difficulty of understanding not only whether associations have value, but also what *value* might mean in this context. The guide to understanding the meaning of value was to combine ordinary opinions about common benefits with a notion of how associations serve collective interests. Value was asked about and uncovered in more or less commonsensical terms.

Improving the performance and safety of products and services, raising standards of professional excellence, and increasing individuals' capacity to assume and exercise responsibility are good things, almost all would say. They are among the practical anchors of everyday life and do not normally need theoretical defense. The discussion to follow, therefore, centers around these concepts, using them to examine whether and precisely how associations are valuable.

Even if associations provide broad societal value, one must still ask how and when countervailing costs reduce it. One must also explore the link between public value and the private collective interests that associations serve. Why are associations, rather than other social or political institutions, necessary or especially useful in doing what they do?

The orientation these concepts and questions provide, together with the research data, suggest that associations provide public value in a number of areas. Discussing where and how, citing examples, and considering associated costs are the substance of this book.

"Responsible collective interests are firmer grounds for public benefit than altruism alone."

Providing Needed Information

The public value of associations is largely a consequence of their intelligent pursuit of collective interest. The fraternity and, especially, the education that associations provide are in their members' interests. Associations enable their members to improve their work by perfecting old techniques and learning new ones. The successful practices of one hospital, for example, can be adapted in other hospitals, raising general levels of technique and service. This diffusion of innovation also improves the services delivered to patients, that is, to the general public. Improved practice increases the skill and efficiency of the professionals or producers who associate and at the same time improves services to the general public.

When an association forms or meets to respond to government or the press, it pursues a collective interest to deal with actual or potential collective treatment. Pursued fairly, such collective responses can improve the legal or public environment in which an industry, profession, or cause operates by providing information and argument that allows government and the media to more realistically assess costs, benefits, and subtle interrelationships. The public interest, as represented in sound government or sound public opinion, is enhanced.

Clearly, collective interest pushed to its extreme is harmful; so is individual selfishness. But collective interest "rightly understood," in the sense of Tocqueville, will appreciate and protect the political and public conditions that this nation values in common, just as individual interest does.

Indeed, much of America's public good is constituted by the common institutions that spell out and enforce justice, free political choice, and national security. Within this political and legal framework, the public interest is further served by the pursuit of individual and collective interests that provide health, wealth, knowledge, and artistic expression. The public as a whole benefits from a climate that allows the pursuit of interest to result in the production of desirable goods. Public law and public opinion, therefore, should respond to reasonable collective interests and individual concerns, in order to protect the remarkable ability of a system based on the pursuit of interest to produce wealth and alleviate poverty.

An airline industry that lobbies to prevent over-regulation, for example, can help government see where laws could create harm. An industry or charity concerned only with its interests, however, can distort public expenditures or private markets so that it is favored too much or controlled too little or so that government attention to common justice, choice, and security is lost in the clash of interests.

Collective interests "rightly understood" and limited by good sense and law, then, serve a public political interest in two ways. First, they provide the information and mobilized strength of members that prevent government from excessively limiting the pursuit of private interest and, therefore, the production of broadly desired goods or services. Second, associations can help articulate, protect, and generate the public conditions of democratic political choice and a subtle understanding of the common good by limiting the tendency of government or of other private interests to dominate if left unchecked.

"Associations of all types call forth extraordinary amounts of volunteer labor."

Supporting a Healthy Marketplace

Associations represent the collective interests of those who produce goods and services. Broadly speaking, the market for any good or service depends on its reputation. Does the air conditioner cool, the physician heal, or the rail system transport smoothly and on time? With many goods, it is difficult to separate the reputation of any single brand from that of the generic product. Not just one item, for example, but all products sold directly or door to door can be tarred by a single unscrupulous salesperson. Consumers, moreover, often cannot independently obtain sufficient advance knowledge to purchase services intelligently and confidently. Consider, for example, how difficult it would be to know in advance who is an adequate physician were there no standards, licenses, and degrees. Nor are individual consumers in any position to demand the coordination of transportation services, products, and parts necessary to move them smoothly from one city to another. And without this coordination, many producers of transportation would find it difficult to sell their products.

In a similar vein, consider the vast number of charities and causes in which citizens may become involved. To enable the public to make informed decisions and to guard against "look-alike" organizations, cause-related groups have erected a number of umbrella groups that maintain standards and provide information covering the activities of charitable groups.[4]

Dealing with the general conditions that affect products, services, and markets are the obvious functions of associations, many of which originate to meet these needs. Meeting these needs affords public value as well. Consumers need information about qualifications, confidence in the reliability and effectiveness of products, and standards for safe and efficient performance as much as producers do. These needs are often complementary. This social value does not come without potential costs that are formally recognized in antitrust laws and economic theory, but the costs do not obviate the value.

The collective interest of producers and providers in the reputation of their products and services is connected to their interest in producing or selling their products and services in common. Associations of agricultural producers, for example, try to ensure that government purchases or supports their products.

Associating for the purpose of collective "producing" or "selling" is also quite common to many charities and causes. Government or private funds, for example, can be collected to research many diseases (that is, prospective research can be "sold" and "purchased") more effectively by an association than by separate individuals. In a sense, the system allowing tax deductions and permitting institutions to receive tax-free gifts is a way the people collectively secure goods (art, research, and education) that they believe the government cannot, should not, or chooses not to provide sufficiently.

Charitable, and to some degree cause-related, associations are private providers or organizers of the production of such goods. They lobby government to fund or support the arts or research, for example. In this sense, charitable associations are not different from any other government supplicant. Indeed, what they want from government and the public can clash with what other charities want or with other public interests. Still, because the "goods" they pursue are so regularly enjoyed by nonmembers, as well as members, their collective motives are not simply self-interested.

"Associations are places where one sees beyond self-interest."

Reaching Out to Others

Many areas of public value are directly connected to and flow from private collective interests, generously or responsibly understood. There is another broad area of public value that is less a twin of the private collective interests that cause people to associate than a consequence of associations' existence. This category is community service and includes the responsibility and self-government that are by-products of volunteering and leadership.

When people offer community service through their associations, they sometimes tie the activity to the original purpose for associating, but other times and more frequently, they provide services outside their immediate scope. The acts of associating and serving other collective interests create additional mechanisms for community service, as well as additional reasons for engaging in it.

Associations of all types call forth extraordinary amounts of volunteer labor. This labor is used to run and manage the association, to participate in association-sponsored education programs, and to set a variety of standards. Volunteer boards are active participants in associations and volunteer experts contribute significant amounts of time and energy to countless committees.

The result is that associations offer significant forums for self-government and the assumption of responsibility beyond the neighborhood, yet short of the state. Associations are places where one sees beyond self-interest, even if only to pursue a collective private interest. And because collective private interest "reasonably understood" often serves the public interest, associations can be places in which to articulate and pursue the public interest.

In the same sense, associations offer solid training grounds for leadership and self-government. Volunteering and providing community service through associations are beneficial to society because these activities help develop and give expression to habits of character and thought devoted to larger public concerns, but from a healthy and realistic base of collective private interest. Indeed, associations provide an arena for altruism which need not undercut the competitive roots of society as a whole.

ENDNOTES

1. The Hudson Institute's survey was conducted on a random, stratified sample of associations drawn from an ASAE list of more than 5,800 associations with staff who were current ASAE members or prospective members. The criterion used to include an association in the survey population was that the organization must have had at least one full-time professional staff member. More than 300 associations were excluded on this basis. The final population from which the survey sample was selected numbered approximately 5,500 organizations.

   Two waves of survey mailings were sent in 1989 to a total of 2,836 potential respondents. Of these, 505 surveys were completed and returned in usable form. Because this was a relatively low response rate, careful checks were made to ensure there were sufficient responses in each stratum, so that the results by stratum, as well as in aggregate, would represent the population at a confidence level of +/- five percent.

   The sample was stratified by three organizational types and four sizes of employment. The organizational types were professional, trade, and cause-related and advocacy associations. For purposes of the overall analysis, the difference among organizational types was more relevant than among employment size, so the data are aggregated by size class within organizational type. Unless otherwise stated, the data presented here are not raw survey data but, rather, have been weighted to produce estimates covering the association universe.

2. ASAE's membership comprises executives from nearly 8,800 trade associations and individual membership organizations.

3. For example, when reported that 88 percent of the surveyed trade and 93 percent of the surveyed professional associations

educate their members, these numbers hold for the full universe of trade and professional associations within the limits discussed. However, when reported that 80 percent of cause-related and advocacy organizations educate their members, the figure accurately reflects a significant part of the universe but not all of it.

4. These groups include the National Health Council, New York; the National Assembly of National Voluntary Health and Social Welfare Organizations, Washington, D.C.; and the American Association of Fund-Raising Counsel, New York.

 # Direct and Indirect Economic Impacts

KEY FINDINGS

- The net direct and indirect economic impact of the surveyed associations is almost $48 billion annually.
- Association employment is at least equal to the employment rolls in such major U.S. industries as steel, computing equipment, communications equipment, or the airlines.
- The professional societies surveyed spend more than $4 billion a year on socially beneficial activities, which include setting standards for education, training, performance, and ethics.
- The cause-related and advocacy organizations surveyed spend almost $3 billion a year to benefit the public. Two-thirds of this sum represents volunteer time, conservatively valued.
- Among the surveyed trade associations, almost $4.5 billion is spent yearly, with significant amounts devoted to research, statistics, and education.
- Associations produce estimated economic impacts ranging from $19 to $24 billion a year in the local economies where they are headquartered.

"Associations'

overall annual net

economic impact

is almost

$48 billion."

Accoding to recent estimates the American not-for-profit sector had at its disposal over $400 billion in resources in 1986. While this includes about $100 billion in the imputed value of volunteer time, it is, nonetheless, an impressive total.[1]

At the same time, the nonprofit sector employed more than 7.7 million people—about one of every 14 wage earners in the nation—paying almost $124 billion in wages and benefits and spending more than $50 billion on goods and services.[2] While these numbers are relatively small when compared to those of the for-profit sector, nonprofits are clearly a major presence in the American economy, representing about 6 percent of the Gross National Product.

Virginia Hodgkinson and M.S. Weitzman, of the Independent Sector, estimate that there are almost 1.3 million nonprofit organizations, of which some 873,000 are philanthropic and 370,000, nonphilanthropic.[3] M.S. O'Neill has suggested a simple taxonomy for these organizations, comprising nine categories that correspond to their principal activities: religion, education and research, health care, arts and culture, social services, advocacy and legal services, international assistance, grant making, and mutual benefit.[4] While this classification is descriptively useful, it is hardly definitive and may add more confusion than clarity when one attempts to deal with theoretical issues, analytical questions, or public policy problems pertinent to not-for-profits. For example, the taxonomy does not deal effectively with gray areas, which are of special concern here, as when a substantial portion of an organization's activities benefit society at large. The American Bar Association exemplifies the problems with O'Neill's scheme. Categorized as a mutual benefit organization, that is, an organization that exists primarily to serve its own members, the association devotes a significant portion of its resources to the public's benefit, through activities like setting codes of ethics and professional standards.

Indeed, much of the literature on the not-for-profit sector suffers from similar shortcomings that arise in part because authors attempt to deal with the whole sector, become overwhelmed by the scope of the task, and must resort to generalities or focus narrowly on one type of not-for-profit organization and usually lose sight of issues pertaining across the board.

This study attempts to avoid these pitfalls by focusing on a subset of not-for-profits and examining their activities in some detail. The subset comprises trade associations, professional associations, and cause-related and advocacy associations. Associations were separated from schools, churches, hospitals, theatre groups, and many other kinds of not-for-profits in order to understand more thoroughly their economic contributions.

The literature was examined on the general economic place of not-for-profits because the notion is incorrect that associations are essentially mutual aid societies which are not especially beneficial to society. These organizations bring together thousands and even millions of individuals to serve their own common purposes and often to serve broader societal ends.

The overall net direct and indirect economic impact of associations represented in the Hudson Institute survey is almost $48 billion. This sum comprises

- almost $9.7 billion in direct cash outlays to conduct operations and provide services;
- $3.3 billion worth of estimated volunteer time expended by members in carrying out association activities;
- $19.9 billion spent by association members on education and training activities and in setting and meeting professional and product and service standards;
- approximately $15 billion in multiplier effects on local economies beyond direct expenditures in the areas in which associations operate.

These figures, large though they are, do not represent the full economic impact of associations; rather, they represent the sum of the partial impacts estimated, using survey techniques and conservative applications of economic theory and empirical practice. More importantly, the figures do not represent the full value of associations in American society because much of that value accrues from the institutional roles these organizations play.

ASSOCIATIONS' ROLE IN THE MARKET ECONOMY

The place of associations within the market economy is difficult to analyze. The roles of regular participants in the marketplace—buyers, producers, providers of capital, workers, and others—are relatively well understood and accepted in the academic literature, making it possible to quantify their contributions, at least approximately. In the case of associations, this is not true.

The principal reason for this inability is that the economic theory of firms and markets, as it is usually taught, requires a variety of simplifying assumptions to be made. These assumptions allow one to ignore the true complexities of the marketplace. In the real world, however, those complexities must be dealt with as real issues involving real people, either as individuals or often in association with one another.

For the market system to operate properly, an extensive list of assumptions must be met. Two of the most important involve the behavior of consumers when they make purchases. First, consumers must be able to obtain and evaluate information on product prices and characteristics in order to determine their preferences. If the information available in the marketplace is inadequate or too technical, some means must be developed to help consumers obtain and evaluate it. The second assumption acknowledges that consumers must bear the full costs and realize the full benefits of their purchases if they are to reveal their true preferences. If some or all of the costs or benefits accrue to others, then a mechanism must be established that appropriately reapportions the costs or benefits. A variety of institutions, some private and some public, have been created to deal with these issues.

Some examples may serve to illustrate. In basic microeconomic theory, consumers are assumed to either have or be able to obtain at no cost all of the information they need to evaluate the suitability of products they consider purchasing. In the real world, this is rarely, if ever, the case; rather, consumers often have very little access to objective information about the products they purchase. An item as commonplace as engine oil may have 10 or 15 critically important physical characteristics, such as sheer strength, viscosity, and detergent properties, that determine its suitability for a given engine under specific conditions of use. Few people who buy engine oil know what these characteristics are, why they are important, how they are measured, or how to compare relative measures of performance. Even fewer know how to conduct tests to measure these characteristics. If one were to depend solely on the competing claims of the dozens of companies manufacturing this product, the end result would almost certainly be one of confusion rather than enlightenment. Obtaining comprehensive, objective information for even this one item would be an expensive, time-consuming, and technically daunting task.

The mechanism that has evolved for dealing with this particular exception to assumptions of the market model involves the cooperation of vehicle manufacturers, oil companies, and an association, the Society of Automotive Engineers (SAE), Warrendale, Pennsylvania. Vehicle manufacturers design their products, keeping in mind certain technical specifications for appropriate lubricants. SAE develops objective methods for testing product characteristics and provides a quick and easy way for consumers to understand the test results. Oil companies conduct those tests on their products, subject to verification, and publish the results on product packages. Then, by comparing the vehicle manufacturers' specifications given in every car owner's manual, a consumer can determine by a fairly straightforward process whether a given brand and type of oil is appropriate for his or her vehicle. This process ensures that consumers can obtain at least the minimum objective information required to make informed and appropriate choices at little or no cost. Of course, companies still spend enormous sums on advertising to provide additional information intended to influence choice, but the value of information from the testing process probably far exceeds the total advertising sum.

Similarly, it is very difficult for a nonprofessional to judge the qualifications of medical, dental, architectural, engineering, and many other practitioners. Associations take a very active role in certifying training programs, establishing standards of practice and ethics, and working with government agencies to ensure regulation of their professions. These efforts enable nonprofessionals to know that those they hire meet at least certain minimum standards as established by their peers. Cause-related and advocacy groups perform similar services in helping the public sift through the enormous array of competing benefits in order to determine which should be addressed. In both examples, were it left solely to the individual consumer to obtain and evaluate such information, the cost of doing so—or the potential cost of being unable to do so—would be enormous.

"There are almost 1.3 million nonprofit organizations."

CALCULATING ASSOCIATIONS' ECONOMIC VALUE

As noted, the theory of market behavior assumes that for the market to work properly, the benefits must accrue fully to consumers, as must the costs. If benefits accrue to others, then the prices consumers bid would be lower than otherwise warranted. Producers would offer less of the product in response to these price signals. Conversely, if there are external costs that consumers cannot be made to bear, then they will receive benefits they are not paying for.

In either case, the market produces inefficient results if left to its own devices. It may, for example, fail to provide enough of some desirable good. The public sector can often improve outcomes in such "market failures" by judiciously applying its powers to regulate, tax, and spend. At times, though, the collective preferences of public markets, as expressed politically, do not satisfy the needs, desires, and choices of all individuals and groups in society. In these cases, other forms of collective action, often expressed through nongovernmental organizations and associations, may provide the means to satisfy those needs. Associations can offer services that smooth the operation of markets and provide or subsidize important activities that might not otherwise be available in a pure market economy.

The fact that so many desirable association activities arise in just those areas where costs and benefits cannot be precisely assigned helps explain the difficulty in precisely calculating associations' economic value. In the case of engine oil, many benefits of a standardized program of testing and grading accrue to the auto manufacturer, which is likely to incur fewer customer complaints and warranty claims if its customers use the oil according to vehicle design specifications. But benefits also accrue to the lubricant manufacturer, who can use this information as a marketing tool, and to the consumer.

It is not immediately clear in this instance who receives the greatest benefit or bears the greatest portion of the cost. Ultimately, it is probably the consumer, because manufacturers could almost certainly develop comparable information in other ways for their own ends and pass most of their costs on to consumers. Such costs would be so well buried in prices that consumers could not possibly distinguish them from other costs. Nor is there any way for consumers to demonstrate what they would willingly pay for oil that includes this information, compared to what they would willingly pay for oil that did not (that is, the marginal price difference for the "enhanced" product), because all major auto and lubricant manufacturers participate in the program. Absent such a choice in the marketplace, consumers' true preferences can neither be revealed, nor the direct economic value of the service ascertained.

The value of professional training courses offered by associations accrues both to the person being trained and to the employer; the value of professional certification accrues both to the certified practitioner and the user of that practitioner's service; the same could be said of almost all association services and activities. In these cases, the true economic value of association functions to society cannot be precisely determined because of the lack of reliable price signals in the market.

Indeed, even if one could determine the prices that beneficiaries of association services were willing to pay and if one could assign the economic value as the sum of all the values that accrue to any beneficiary, one still could not state the total value in precise operational terms. This is so because there is no effective way to segregate that element in the price of many products and services which represents the value of benefits. Indeed, associations often give away their benefits. Doing so in no way detracts from the economic value of associations, but points to the difficulty of precisely measuring it.

Of course, not all association activities are of uncompromised economic benefit. In some cases the economic costs are ill-understood and difficult to measure. For example, in the past, some trade associations and professional groups have engaged in activities that have adversely affected competition in certain markets. This influence has taken the form of limiting entry to a business or profession, apportioning markets, or in other ways placing the group members in a position to derive some benefit they would not otherwise receive in an open, competitive market. In the language of economists, those who gain from limited competition enjoy monopoly rents, that is, they enjoy the excess of what they earn in noncompetitive markets, compared with what they would have earned in markets with free entry and enhanced competition.

In some cases, such as medicine, there is general consensus that the public benefits of limiting professional entry to licensed practitioners and allowing practitioners to have some influence in establishing credentials and licensing procedures are worth the cost. This consensus is recognized in law and public policy. In other cases, activities that limit competition have been found illegal under antitrust laws. Even activities that enjoy general legal protections, such as setting product standards, have in a few cases proved to be illegal in practice when

"Community service, education, public information, and research and statistics account for more than half of all association spending."

the activity limits competition without an offsetting public benefit.

Clearly, this economic calculus involves an extraordinarily complex process of identifying and valuing benefits or costs that are often subtle, difficult to measure, and virtually impossible to attribute to any single individual or firm. As a result, such costs and benefits do not appear as identifiable categories in standard economic statistics.

All of this makes clear that putting hard numbers to a concept as complex as the economic value of associations—especially when the theoretical rules of the market economy do not clearly apply—is a daunting task. To circumvent these complexities, Hudson researchers took a different approach by gathering information on association spending in providing services as a first-order approximation of the economic value of those services. Two caveats applied: (1) recognition that information is merely a proxy for the real value of association services, for the reasons previously noted and (2) that such data inform neither about the distribution of economic benefits, nor about the economic costs of these activities. The economic value of associations, therefore, is described in terms of the functions they perform, following the work of the institutionalist school of economics and the other noneconomic analyses in this report.

THE SURVEY RESULTS

The data for the study came from a survey of a randomly selected, stratified sample of associations. A total of 505 usable surveys were returned from two mailings, for a response rate of approximately 20 percent at a confidence interval of + / - 5 percent.[5]

The estimate of the total, direct annual cash expenditures of associations in the survey population is $9.691 billion, of which trade associations account for more than 45 percent, professional associations more than 43 percent, and cause-related and advocacy groups 10.5 percent. These associations marshal more than 330 million hours of volunteer time each year in carrying out their activities. Valued conservatively at $10 per hour, this time represents in excess of another $3.3 billion, almost 60 percent of which is directly attributable to the cause-related and advocacy organizations. The combined total dollar value of these resources, some $13 billion, represents the total resources that the reporting associations marshal to conduct their activities and provide services to their members, other constituents, and the public. Table 1 presents this information in greater detail.[6]

Table 1 **Association Expenditures**
(in $ millions)

Association Type	Direct Expenditures	Volunteer Hours		Total Combined Value
		Number	Value*	
Trade	$4,428.6	19.1	$ 191.2	$ 4,619.8
Professional	4,243.8	118.0	1,180.2	5,424.0
Cause-related and advocacy	1,019.0	195.6	1,956.2	2,975.2
Total**	$9,691.4	332.7	$3,327.6	$13,019.0

*Volunteer hours are valued at $10 per hour.
**The slight differences in totals among tables are due to rounding.

To note the distribution of association expenditures by the type of activity or service provided, see table 2. Associations spend about $1 in every $4 on administration or fund-raising. These expenditures are included with those which have public benefit because without them associations could not exist and other expenditures that have more direct societal benefit could not be made.

Community service, education programs, public information, and research and statistical analysis account for more than half of all association spending. Another 6.8 percent goes to quasi-regulatory functions, and the balance is spent on conventions and political education.

The associations surveyed employ almost 500,000 full-time equivalent employees. The volunteer hours their members contribute represent about another 170,000 full-time equivalents. Based on paid staff alone, association employment is at least equal to the employment rolls in such major U.S. industries as steel, computing equipment, communications equipment, or the airlines.[7] Cause-related and advocacy groups employ the bulk of paid association staff and generate almost 60 percent of the full-time equivalent volunteer staff, with most of the rest from professional groups. Professional associations dominate trade associations by a wide margin in the number of personnel resources available to devote to activities (table 3).

Table 2 Association Expenditures by Function
(in $ millions)

Function	Direct Expenditures	Value of Volunteer Hours*	Total $	Total Percent
Administration and fund-raising	$2,777.6	$ 562.9	$ 3,340.5	25.7 %
Research and statistics	2,063.9	67.0	2,130.9	16.4
Education programs	1,423.3	629.6	2,052.9	15.8
Community service	784.8	976.7	1,761.5	13.5
Public information	769.6	543.2	1,312.8	10.1
Conventions	872.6	263.4	1,136.0	8.7
Political education	360.8	30.2	391.0	3.0
Setting performance and safety standards	282.9	94.3	377.2	2.9
Setting ethical standards	71.3	68.4	139.7	1.1
Setting professional standards	90.1	17.0	107.1	0.8
Certifying professional standards	83.9	23.8	107.7	0.8
Certifying performance and safety standards	62.8	5.3	68.1	0.5
Enforcing ethical standards	29.8	37.8	67.6	0.5
Accreditation	17.7	7.8	25.5	0.2
Total**	$9,691.1	$3,327.4	$13,018.5	100.0

*Volunteer hours are valued at $10 per hour.
**The slight differences in totals among tables are due to rounding.

Table 3 Human Resources of Associations

Association Type	Professional Staff*	Volunteers Number*	Volunteers Hours
Trade	53,958	9,560	19,170
Professional	88,920	59,010	118,020
Cause-related and advocacy	357,077	97,810	195,620
Total	499,955	166,380	

*Expressed in full-time equivalent positions, each measured at 2,000 hours per full-time equivalent year (40-hour work week × 50 weeks worked a year = 2,000 hours).

Professional associations represent more than two-thirds of the total dues-paying members in the survey population, or 115.7 million people. Cause-related and advocacy groups represent 40.2 million, for a grand total of almost 166 million members, and trade associations represent 10.3 million member companies.[8]

A figure worth noting is the more than $5.3 billion that trade and professional association members spend to take education and training programs which they attribute to association efforts or requirements (table 4). Clearly, association-set standards add greatly to members' motivations to pursue education and training; the efforts of associations contribute to the availability and usefulness of educational programs. Thus, while associations cannot control all of their members' expenditures for education and training, it is not unreasonable to include this sum when totaling economic impact.

Table 4 **Expenditures of Association Members**
(in $ millions)

Association Type	Education and Training	Meeting Standards
Trade	$1,950.3	$ 8,840.0
Professional	3,078.8	5,631.1
Cause-related and advocacy	313.0	100.5
Total*	$5,342.1	$14,571.6

*The slight differences in totals among tables are due to rounding.

A parallel argument can be made regarding members' expenditures in meeting standards. This massive sum, in excess of $14.5 billion, suggests quite forcefully just how seriously the business and professional communities in this country take their responsibilities—responsibilities strongly encouraged and actively supported by many of the associations surveyed (table 4).

It is clear that, in aggregate, associations command enormous resources, financial and human. The use of those resources and their economic value to society will be discussed next.

PROFESSIONAL ASSOCIATIONS
Benefits to Members

According to the dictionary, a profession is a calling or occupation requiring specialized knowledge that often necessitates long, intensive academic preparation. This definition is inadequate for the purposes of this study, especially at a time when more and more jobs fit this overly broad rubric. Some other characteristics also distinguish a profession from other forms of employment.

- A practitioner must meet certain requirements during education and training that demonstrate specific proficiency.
- The practitioner's work may have a profound effect on the safety, health, or well-being of the client or employer.
- Detailed knowledge of the profession is required to evaluate candidates' qualifications and to judge existing practitioners' competency.
- A practitioner shares a body of knowledge, professional techniques, and common interests that ally him or her more closely with others in the profession than with clients or employers.

These requirements tend to drive professionals into association with one another, spurring them to seek common advantages, including freedom from nonprofessionals in the practice of their profession and limitations on entry to the profession. The special status of professionals is often codified into law, and many professions are given the full weight of legal protection. This status is often heightened by state requirements that practitioner candidates be certified or licensed to practice and by legal sanctions of criminal prosecution for those who attempt to practice without appropriate credentials.

Legal recognition of the unique qualities and conditions of professional practice confers on practitioners many advantages. In purely economic terms, the most important of these is the barrier to entry that is almost always created when a profession gains recognition. Such barriers may limit the supply of the relevant professional service but have no equivalent effect on demand. The straightforward result in a market where supply is constrained from changing in response to demand is that the price of the service tends to vary more or less directly with demand; that is, as demand rises, so does the price the practitioner can charge. It is, therefore, not surprising that in simple economic terms many groups seek formal recognition as a profession.

The effectiveness of barriers to professional entry varies a great deal, based on such factors as the stringency of educational requirements, the difficulty of the certification or licensing procedure (whether a test is required, for example, and if so, what sort), the practitioners' degree of control in accrediting training programs and influencing certification or licensing procedures, and the level of legal enforcement. It is vastly more difficult to become a physician in this country than to become a cosmetologist, though both professions are regulated. In large part that derives from the nature of the activities and their impact on public safety and health, but it also derives from the effectiveness of medical associations in dealing with the process by which new doctors are trained and certified.

Other benefits may also accrue to practitioners of a recognized profession. They are often accorded great autonomy in establishing standards of ethics and practice and in enforcing those standards for all members, usually with relatively little interference from legal authorities. The visibility, credibility, and resources of an organized profession also often give it political influence disproportionate to its numbers. Many professionals enjoy elevated social status merely by nature of their occupations.

Benefits to Society

Because recognized professionals receive such benefits, it is reasonable to ask what society receives in return for these protections and privileges.[9] Foremost, consumers of professional services, virtually all of whom lack adequate information to judge the ability and performance of a practitioner, are assured the practitioner has met standards for education and training, performance, and ethics established by those who do have adequate information to make such judgments, namely, the practitioner's peers. When the system of peer regulation works, it is tremendously beneficial to society, because employment of a professional practitioner almost always involves some degree of significant risk. The greater and more crucial the risk, the more an individual consumer would presumably be willing to pay to obtain information that would allow him or her to minimize or eliminate it.

Society also benefits from any improvements in the quality of professional practice. One effective way of ensuring that new information and innovative techniques are disseminated is to encourage cooperation among professionals in mutual learning endeavors. Professionals are responsible for directing and conducting research that upgrades standards of practice and for publishing or otherwise disseminating information to other practitioners, as well as to interested consumers.

The nature of most professional practices, however, makes it difficult to enforce expectations on individual practitioners, since they typically operate independently or in relatively small groups and with limited individual resources. Thus, while most professional practitioners would acknowledge the benefits they receive by way of society's recognition, they as individuals have difficulty meeting the reciprocal social obligations they incur. A practical approach has evolved to deal with this dilemma by utilizing the institutional structure invariably created early in the process of organizing and establishing a profession—the professional association.

No professional association would be able to indefinitely secure for its member the recognition and benefits of professional status were it not to meet the responsibilities that society expects. Professional associations at the national, state, and local levels serve as vehicles through which resources can be accumulated and applied most effectively in satisfying those responsibilities.

Resource Expenditures

In 1989, the professional associations surveyed accumulated and spent in excess of $4 billion on socially beneficial activities. In addition, their members contributed 117 million hours of volunteer service, valued conservatively at almost $1.2 billion (table 5).

Major resource expenditures worth noting include more than $1 billion for professional education programs, more than $780 million for community service, and a combined total of $574 million for all types of regulatory functions, including setting, certifying, and enforcing professional, ethical, performance, and safety standards. Other significant outlays were made for public information research and statistical analysis.

As noted in table 4, professional association members made huge direct expenditures to further the aims of their associations in promoting the highest levels of education and strict adherence to standards. During the survey period, they spent an estimated $3.1 billion on education and training. Only one state in the nation, California, spends more to support public higher education. This significant figure is equivalent to more than 10 percent of all state appropriations for higher education.

The expenditures of professional association members in meeting and enforcing professional standards represents another $5.6 billion. While much of this is spent on meeting standards (for example, taking certification

Table 5 Professional Association Expenditures by Function
(in $ millions)

Function	Direct Expenditures	Value of Volunteer Hours*	Total $	Percent
Administration and fund-raising	$1,493.5	$ 226.9	$1,720.4	31.7%
Education programs	715.2	315.0	1,030.2	19.0
Community service	691.3	89.1	780.4	14.4
Conventions	443.2	185.1	628.3	11.6
Public information	265.4	90.7	356.1	6.6
Setting performance and safety standards	159.4	79.9	239.3	4.4
Research and statistics	168.8	55.4	224.2	4.1
Setting ethical standards	31.6	61.3	92.9	1.7
Political education	78.9	6.4	85.3	1.6
Setting professional standards	60.2	10.3	70.5	1.3
Certifying professional standards	44.6	13.8	58.4	1.1
Certifying performance and safety standards	55.0	4.1	59.1	1.1
Enforcing ethical standards	19.7	34.5	54.2	1.0
Accreditation	17.1	7.7	24.8	0.5
Total**	$4,243.9	$1,180.2	$5,424.1	100.0

*Volunteer hours are valued at $10 per hour.
**The slight differences in totals among tables are due to rounding.

examinations or fulfilling apprenticeships and internships), rather than on regulatory efforts, expenditures such as these may translate the most directly into benefits for consumers and society at large.

CAUSE-RELATED AND ADVOCACY ORGANIZATIONS

The role of cause-related and advocacy organizations in society is harder to explicate in economic terms than the roles of the other two types of associations. The two other types of associations were formed to serve their members' economic interests and proved to be convenient institutional vehicles for providing public value. In most cases, the cause-related and advocacy organizations do not serve their members' immediate economic interests. Indeed, in many cases, those who benefit most from their activities are not members at all. Relatively few members of health associations, such as the American Cancer Society, the Muscular Dystrophy Association, and the American Heart Association, are patients currently afflicted with those diseases; rather, they are health professionals, ex-patients, family members of patients, or, most frequently, concerned laypeople interested in serving a worthy cause. In purely economic terms, it is difficult to explain the commitment these members make to their causes. The same can be said of members of the many fraternal and benevolent associations also included in this category.

It is possible to gain some insights into the social contributions these organizations make by examining their activities. In many cases, these activities are public services that public agencies do not perform or do not perform to the satisfaction of a given association's members.

By its nature, a public good or service cannot be provided efficiently through normal markets. Because the benefits of a public good do not accrue solely to the purchaser and because nonpurchasers cannot be excluded from enjoying the benefits, a public good left to private markets usually results in a pricing mechanism failure and undersupply of the good. One might expect government, using its power to tax, to completely provide public goods. But government is legally prevented from providing some such goods, would insufficiently provide still others, and in a liberal democracy private provision is desirable.

Many people of religious conviction, for example, believe strongly that education should embody a religious component. Although public education is readily available, and in most cases adequately funded, government is prohibited from teaching religion. The answer has been establishment of educational institutions with religious affiliations. Often, however, the cost of running these institutions is so high that, were students required to pay tuition, this type of education would be beyond the reach of all but a few. Therefore, support of the religious organization, and often that of a group formed to generate financial support for the institution and its students, replaces the public subsidy that students in public institutions receive.

"Often, those who benefit most from cause-related organizations are not members at all."

The list of public or quasi-public causes promoted through the efforts of groups and associations is long and varied. They range from fine arts groups, to associations promoting research and education in specific diseases, from those concerned with environmental issues, to those focusing on amateur sports. Some of these organizations concentrate on raising funds for their causes, others on securing the members' direct personal involvement. Some support institutions, others work for the benefit of individuals. Some are nationwide in scope, others may be organized in a single neighborhood. Some, such as fraternal organizations, may even be regarded as "generalist" organizations that may promote more than one cause simultaneously or sequentially, as the members' perceptions and concerns change. The most important features all these groups share is a concern about a public matter and a desire to associate with others of like concern to take collective action on the matter.

The resources these associations bring to bear on issues, while relatively small in comparison to those of the government, may be significantly out of proportion to their size. For example, the research and public information activities sponsored by the March of Dimes contributed tremendously to the development and virtually universal use of vaccines to prevent polio, with the result that children born after the late 1950s have almost no chance of being victims. The public information activities of various consumer and environmental groups have done a great deal to provide useful counterpoint to other interests in discussions and public debates, leading in a number of cases to significant changes in law or public policy.

Resource Expenditures

There are many such examples that show the exceptional effectiveness of many of these organizations, despite their limited resources. One reason for this success is that members are often quite knowledgeable about the cause in question or are extremely dedicated or both. The skills and enthusiasm such people bring to these associations is probably significantly understated when arbitrarily valued at $10 per hour, but there is no practical way to determine a better figure.[10] Thus, the 200 million or more volunteer hours mobilized by the surveyed organizations could represent far more than the assigned $2 billion value were these volunteers receiving salaries.

The total resources of the advocacy and cause-related associations in the survey is some $2.97 billion, of which about one-third represents actual cash outlays, with the remainder composed of volunteer time.[11]

These organizations' reliance on volunteers is significant (table 6). For example, they devote about twice as much volunteer time to conventions as direct expenditures. Approximately 80 percent of the volunteer efforts are utilized to provide direct services, such as education programs, public information, political education, and community service, while about half of all cash outlays are used for these purposes.

More than 70 percent of the combined cash and volunteer resources is used for information, education, and community service activities, while about 20 percent is used for administration and fund-raising. The only other expenditure category of any significance is conventions, on which these associations expended about

Table 6 **Cause-Related and Advocacy Association Expenditures by Function**
(in $ millions)

Function	Direct Expenditures	Value of Volunteer Hours*	Total $	Total Percent
Community service	$ 91.3	$ 884.9	$ 976.2	32.8%
Public information	263.9	407.8	671.7	22.6
Administration and fund-raising	331.8	301.5	633.3	21.3
Education programs	142.1	274.5	416.6	14.0
Conventions	69.8	64.8	134.6	4.5
Research and statistics	49.1	2.2	51.3	1.7
Political education	28.2	6.5	34.7	1.2
Setting performance and safety standards	21.6	2.6	24.2	0.8
Certifying professional standards	14.2	7.6	21.8	0.7
Enforcing ethical standards	2.5	2.7	5.2	0.2
Setting ethical standards	1.8	0.5	2.3	0.1
Certifying performance and safety standards	1.2	0.3	1.5	0.1
Setting professional standards	0.8	0.1	0.9	0.0
Accreditation	0.6	0.3	0.9	0.0
Total**	$1,018.9	$1,956.3	$2,975.2	100.0

*Volunteer hours are valued at $10 per hour.
**The slight differences in totals among tables are due to rounding.

4.5 percent of their resources. Thus, almost $3 billion worth of funds and volunteer time are, in effect, contributed to benefit the public by these advocacy and cause-related groups.

TRADE ASSOCIATIONS

In most cases, trade associations originally formed to promote the economic interests of their members. The early history of these organizations contains some examples of excesses in their efforts to promote those interests. In the name of promoting the health of the business community and often that of a particular industry, association members took cooperative actions that sometimes proved to be restraints on trade, collusion to prevent successful unionization of their labor forces, and other activities that ran counter to an efficiently operating market system. While some nonassociation activities produce the same effects (particularly those limiting new competitors from entering the industry, agreements to stifle technological advances, and market-sharing arrangements), it is the rare industry, indeed, in which the societal benefits gained outweigh the costs. As a result, these activities have long been regarded as questionable.

Over the course of the nation's industrialization, the legal system has developed a body of statute and case law that has outlawed a wide range of activities which some trade associations were once wont to conduct, giving legal recognition to the importance of competition and unrestrained trade in the efficient, equitable operation of a market economy.

This is not to say the early days of all trade associations were primarily an effort to reduce competition and benefit their memberships at society's expense. Many functions these groups performed and still perform are of significant value to the public. The large proportion of trade associations played no role in abuses of the past. Indeed, many of them did not exist when such practices were more common.

Today, though occasional legal violations are still found, they are much less likely to be intentional and much more likely to be an unintended side effect of some generally sanctioned activity, such as when establishment of product safety and performance standards excludes the introduction of some new product without sufficient reason.

"Associations play a quasi-regulatory role when establishing performance and safety standards for products and services."

As institutional actors in the market economy, trade associations play a variety of constructive roles. Many of their functions are similar to those of professional associations: They provide education for their members on scientific and technical matters, business practices, legal issues, environmental concerns, and many other topics where the formal educational structure lacks expertise or is not motivated by market demand to provide such services. This dissemination of information enhances the market posture both of the businesses that receive it and of their customers.

In other cases, trade associations may play a quasi-regulatory role by establishing product performance and safety standards and ethical canons. Voluntary standards reduce the risks that consumers face in the marketplace. These standards may even be given the force of law, as when product standards are written into building codes and employee safety regulations.

Trade associations also often provide valuable information about the workings of their membership. The American Gas Association, Arlington, Virginia; American Petroleum Institute, Washington, D.C.; and Edison Electric Institute, Washington, D.C., provide detailed statistical information about the workings of components within the energy sector. Researchers, regulators, policy makers, consumer groups, and many others use the data to improve their understanding and analysis of the specific markets and member companies. Many trade association sources are often regarded as so authoritative that they are cited in statistical reference materials by the federal government.

Trade associations also play an important role in the real-world economy in promoting the direct interests of their members. The efforts of the Motor Vehicle Manufacturers Association, Detroit, were a significant factor in establishment of voluntary export restraints by Japanese manufacturers. The American Iron and Steel Institute, Washington, D.C., has played an important role in developing anti-dumping regulations designed to hinder the importation of foreign products at artificially low prices. While some may contend that such activities do not ultimately benefit consumers, the purpose of this discussion is to demonstrate that trade associations have far-reaching effects on some members of society other than their members.[12]

Resource Expenditures

The resources expended by trade associations in conducting their activities are primarily direct expenditures, which totaled an estimated $4.4 billion among the survey population in 1989 (table 7). As one might expect, the volunteer hours generated were the smallest among associations, an estimated 19.1 million hours with a total value of approximately $191 million.

More than $4 in every $10 is used to fund or conduct research and develop and analyze statistical data. Beyond the importance of these activities to a wide array of participants, the magnitude of these expenditures clearly highlights the importance that trade association members place on research and statistical functions.

Trade associations also spend significant amounts to educate their members and to provide information to the public—almost $2 in every $10. Approximately 5 percent of their resources are used to develop and enforce product, professional, and ethical standards. While

Table 7 **Trade Association Expenditures by Function**
(in $ millions)

Function	Direct Expenditures	Value of Volunteer Hours*	Total $	Total Percent
Research and statistics	$1,846.1	$ 9.3	$1,855.4	40.2%
Administration and fund-raising	952.4	34.9	987.3	21.4
Education programs	566.1	40.4	606.5	13.1
Conventions	359.6	13.5	373.1	8.1
Public information	240.4	44.6	285.0	6.2
Political education	253.6	17.3	270.9	5.9
Setting performance and safety standards	101.9	11.7	113.6	2.5
Setting ethical standards	37.9	6.7	44.6	1.0
Setting professional standards	29.1	6.6	35.7	0.8
Certifying professional standards	25.1	2.4	27.5	0.6
Certifying performance and safety standards	6.5	1.0	7.5	0.2
Enforcing ethical standards	7.6	0.6	8.2	0.2
Community service	2.2	2.7	4.9	0.1
Accreditation	0.1	0.0	0.1	0.0
Total**	$4,428.6	$191.7	$4,620.3	100.0

*Volunteer hours are valued at $10 per hour.
**The slight differences in totals among tables are due to rounding.

this seems like a small amount given the potential importance of these activities, it represents almost a quarter of a billion dollars.

In one of the most surprising figures to emerge from the study, trade associations spend about 6 percent of their volunteer and cash resources on political education. This represents a nontrivial sum of about $270 million, but the relatively small proportion of funds spent on political activities may give lie to the notion, popular in some circles, that trade associations exist primarily to influence political outcomes.

Trade association members spend an astonishing $8.8 billion on standard setting and enforcement (table 4). While much of this is due to mandatory testing to ensure that products meet government or industry standards (rather than to the promulgation of standards), this entire area is clearly of great importance to the smooth functioning of a consumer-oriented economy.

In some ways, the almost $2 billion amount spent by trade association members on education and training is equally surprising. This amount is almost two-thirds of that spent by members of professional associations, for whom the impact of training is presumably of greater immediate necessity and greater personal gain.

EFFECT ON LOCAL ECONOMIES

Associations also make a major impact on economic conditions in the areas where their offices are located and their meetings and conventions held. In the terminology of regional economists and economic development specialists, association offices can be described as part of the export base of a community, that is, they export many of their services outside of the local area and bring revenues into the local area in exchange for those services. Much of that revenue is then spent in the local community to pay staff or buy the goods and services the association needs to operate. These funds are, in turn, spent by association employees to meet their living expenses or by association suppliers to pay their employees, buy the goods they sell, obtain services, and so on in an ever-widening circle of economic exchange. Thus, the inflow of dollars from outside the community can affect the community's overall level of economic activity in some significant multiple of its original value.

This multiplication of economic activity, also known as a *multiplier effect*, has a similar impact on employment.

The creation of one job in an export-type activity results in creation of some greater number of additional jobs in a local economy.

There is broad consensus, supported by empirical tests, that this multiplier effect does exist, but just how big it is remains the subject of some debate. In part, the value of the multiplier depends on the self-sufficiency of the local economy. For example, an association head-quartered in New York, Washington, D.C., or Chicago is much more likely to be able to meet most of its needs for specialized services and some basic goods from local sources, than an association whose offices are located in a small town in the Midwest. Other less predictable factors also come into play, such as employees' spending preferences, the nature of goods and services the associa-tion purchases, and the like. Estimates of the numerical value of this multiplier range from a high of 4 or 5 for a relatively self-sufficient economy (that is, every $1 of revenue generated from outside the economy results in an increase of $4 or $5 in total economic activity within it), to a low of 2 to 2.5. Usually, the actual figure can be estimated for any given local economy by direct empirical testing.

For purposes of this analysis, a figure at the lower end of the range is probably appropriate; even though association offices tend to be found in larger cities, some of the organizations surveyed are local groups whose activities do not generate income from outside the local economy (and thus probably have lesser effects on that economy) and some of the groups are located in smaller, less economically autonomous communities. Even an extremely conservative estimate of the value of the local economic multiplier attributable to associations, say in the range of 2.0 to 2.5, would produce estimated economic impacts ranging from $19 billion to $24 billion in the local economies where they are located.[13,14]

Associations are also very desirable additions to a local economy for reasons other than their direct economic impact. They have little or no impact on the local environ-ment, they make few demands on public sector services, they place little stress on the local infrastructure, and they employ significant numbers of well-educated and well-com-pensated people who are useful members of the community.

ENDNOTES
1. Hodgkinson, V.A. and Weitzman, M.S., *Dimensions of the Indepen-dent Sector: A Statistical Profile; Interim Update: Fall 1988* (Washington, D.C.: Independent Sector, 1988).

2. Ibid.

3. Ibid.

4. O'Neill, M.S., *The Third America: The Emergence of the Nonprofit Sector in the United States*. (San Francisco: Jossey-Bass Publishers, 1989).

5. The survey sample did not include any of the so-called "mega-associations," such as the American Association of Retired Persons with 28 million members. This was not intentional, since the sampling procedure was random and since organizations of such size are rare.

   Noninclusion of "mega-associations" made statistical analysis of the results somewhat easier; these groups are so large that the data they provided would surely have had disproportionate effects on the results, making some adjustment necessary to ensure the end data reflected typical associations.

   Nevertheless, the data clearly understate the overall economic impact and total membership of associations, because the effects of the very large organizations are not included. The understatement is most profound among cause-related and advocacy associations, the category in which the "mega-associations" would have fallen. This understating is further magnified by the fact that ASAE's membership rolls are not comprehensive for cause-related and advocacy groups.

   The data are stronger and more representative of typical associations when apportioning spending among activities than if one or more "mega-associations" had been included. Hudson Institute researchers suggest separate follow-up analysis of these very large groups if it is deemed crucial to include them in subsequent studies.

6. The actual flow of financial resources within the associations surveyed is considerably higher than the figures quoted in table 1. If all of the associations' operating budgets had been included, the total would be almost $25 billion. Because the research focuses on associations' direct value to society, the study excludes such items as capital expenditures, pass-through funds to other organizations or individuals in the form of grants and contributions, and funds expended on programs such as insurance.

7. U.S. Bureau of the Census, *Statistical Abstract of the United States, 1989*, 109th ed. (Washington, D.C.: U.S. Government Printing Office, 1989), 399, 401.

8. While 166 million may seem high, professionals are likely to be members of a number of organizations that represent their interests. This tendency is present among members of other types of associations as well, although it is somewhat less prevalent.

9. Some writers suggest that, along with the well-recognized benefits and the derivative costs to consumers, society must bear another group of costs when a profession is regulated that is not widely recognized. These include lower rates of innovation, unwarranted

protection of practitioners from scrutiny, inappropriate withholding of information regarding qualifications or competency as revealed in licensing or standards enforcement proceedings, and such other practices that tend to put the practitioner's interests ahead of the consumer's.

10. While highly desirable, it is virtually impossible to determine a more accurate figure in work of this nature. Instead, the accepted practice in the literature has been to use the average hourly wage, adjusted upward for benefits. The $10-per-hour figure was chosen, based on a 1989 estimated average hourly rate of $9.25, with a small arbitrary adjustment of approximately 7 percent for benefits. The $10 figure, while perhaps slightly conservative, seems to be substantiative and well within the limits of reason.

11. Volunteers' contributions are a particularly valuable function of cause-related and advocacy associations, since it is highly likely that their time, if not devoted to the associations, would be used in leisure or some other less economically beneficial way. By providing a cause for volunteers, a focus for their activities, and a means of applying their efforts in an effective way, associations add significantly to the total volume of productive activity in the economy.

12. In the cited examples, it could be said that thousands of United Auto Workers, United Steel workers, other unions, retailers, suppliers to large industries, and many others throughout the economic chain supported by these major industries gained from efforts to limit aggressive and, in some cases, unfair competition until the industries were better able to respond in the marketplace.

13. $9.7 million (direct cash outlays) × 2 (multiplier) = $19.4 million; $9.7 million × 2.5 = $24.25 million.

14. Often, associations do not hold meetings and conventions in their local areas, suggesting that local economies where the association offices are located will not reap the benefits of some large portion of total convention expenditures. The locational spending patterns of associations were not identified, making further precision impossible, other than to recognize that the phenomenon exists. This is another reason for a conservative estimate of the local economic multiplier. The multiplier effect of convention expenditures still occurs, but the major effect is seen in communities where meetings and conventions are held, not in those where the association is headquartered.

 # Member and Public Education

KEY FINDINGS

- Associations are more deeply immersed in education than in any other activity, save conventions.
- Association members spend nearly $5.5 billion annually to take educational offerings their associations organize, require, or facilitate.
- Education based in associations serves the public by improving the technical skills and leadership and management abilities of members and nonmembers, which helps to improve services and products.
- Association education provides public value by furnishing general information about goods, services, causes, and public issues.
- The special place of association education is found in translating general discoveries and principles into the concrete requirements of particular industries and professions. This capacity places associations in a potentially leading role to train and retrain the future workforce.
- Association education serves the interests of members by increasing their productivity, enabling them to meet requirements for continuing education, helping to define their profession, and providing an important source of revenue. The public interest is directly related to this self-interest.

"Education is by far the single most prevalent activity among associations, except for administration and conventions."

N o institution, perhaps, is more important than education. Its significance generates a constant barrage of argument and criticism, evaluation and analysis. While the intensity of the debate may vary, it is always vigorous. Over the past decade, Americans have engaged in this discussion with a special urgency. The U.S. Department of Education and the National Endowment for the Humanities have supported studies that document the woeful understanding of American high school students in mathematics, the sciences, and history. Best-selling author Allan Bloom has demonstrated the narrowing of human possibilities that inferior higher education produces, whatever the apparent growth in freedom and wealth.[1]

The U.S. Department of Labor together with the Hudson Institute have spotlighted the impending crisis in workplace literacy: Will a workforce whose literacy has been declining be able to contribute productively in an economy whose literacy requirements are increasing?[2] The consensus is that education in basic skills, advanced technical science and mathematics, and the fundamental works of Western thought all need to be overhauled. The precise end product, means, and strategy for doing this remain at issue, but the necessity does not.

Associations' participation in the educational process is significant. Indeed, they could become an even more important part of the nation's educational restructuring, especially in technical education and workplace literacy.

Offering education programs is by far the single most prevalent activity among associations, save for administration and conventions; it is *the* single most prevalent activity among professional groups. Nearly 90 percent of the associations surveyed offer education programs and services to members. Close to 95 percent of professional associations, 76 percent of trade associations, and more than 80 percent of the cause-related and advocacy organizations are educationally involved.

These figures do not include public education and public information, which also are extremely widespread functions, more prevalent than any other except administration, conventions, and member education. More than 71 percent of the associations surveyed are engaged in public information efforts, comprising 85 percent of cause-related and advocacy groups, 73 percent of trade associations, and 66 percent of professional organizations.

Associations also use volunteers extensively in their education programs, with 84 percent engaging them in member education and more than 61 percent in public education. Taken together, education programs involve over one-third of associations' total volunteer activity.

The educational activity also involves a great deal of money. Adding together member and public education, the surveyed associations spend 26 percent of their total yearly expenditures on education or close to $2.2 billion (using the weighted total expenditure of more than $9 billion). Even this sum, however, understates the total. The surveyed associations estimate their members spend more than $5.3 billion annually in taking education and training programs organized, required, or substantially facilitated by the association. The total association contribution to education, therefore, approaches $8.5 billion annually.

The value of education goes well beyond these numbers. Even if education programs cost associations nothing to offer and their members nothing to take, their utility would be great. One can best discuss these values by differentiating member education and public information and analyzing each systematically.

MEMBER EDUCATION

Advancing the education of their members is a chief benefit that associations bring. The benefit to society flows from the benefit to members, for much association education is designed to improve the members' performance, that is, to improve the delivery of products and services that members create.

Associations comprise groups of people engaged in producing every durable and nondurable product, in husbanding every agricultural and other natural resource, and in producing the whole range of health, business, personal, and professional services. Consumers demonstrate their belief in the worth of these products and services everyday in their purchases. Consequently, consumers' or society's interest in improvements that arise from education can be as great as the interest of members themselves. Associations whose main goal is to further a charity or cause also improve their members' skills through education, consequently expanding their ability to serve the public.

One can divide association's educational efforts into three major areas: technique, leadership and management skills, and ethics and social responsibility. In all of these, improved skills for members permit improved services by members to the public.

Technique

Technique involves mastering the methods necessary to perform specific operations in order to achieve given results. This concept is illuminated most clearly in engineering, medicine, and other scientifically based professions. Teaching techniques also is vital in industries grounded in technological understanding. Indeed, technique is important in any profession or industry where methods can change systemically, even if they are not based on technological developments. Law and education are good examples.

Associations are very important purveyors of technical education. Giving refresher courses, organizing executive education, and providing training workshops are among the activities best known to the public. Their value, quite simply, is that they enable professionals and people in industry to keep up with and use new developments in their work. Associations have an advantage of being able to tailor general knowledge to the specific needs of working professionals, connecting the broad principles or practices that might be taught in a university setting to specific issues in an industry or profession.

One good example of associations' educational efforts is found in medicine. There are 2,000 national medical associations, divided regionally, ethnically, and by specialty, with specialized medical societies offering a striking array of courses, both live and on tape.[3]

The American Academy of Facial Plastic and Reconstructive Surgery, Washington, D.C., for example, offers nearly 200 videotaped courses, ranging from techniques for facelifts, rhinoplasty, and blepharoplasty, to head and neck surgery and the use of lasers. The courses are developed by an association arm or taped at Academy courses and demonstrations.

The Society for Nuclear Medicine, New York, also produces videotapes on technical subjects for nuclear medicine practitioners, physicians in training, technologists, general practitioners, and educators. Most have been

"Nearly 90% of the associations offer education programs and services to members."

produced since 1985, highlighting the utility of associations in keeping members abreast of extraordinarily rapid technical change. "With a new and ever changing technology that is becoming available to nuclear medicine professionals, a need has arisen for more advanced continuing education," according to Society literature.[4]

The utility of technical training in medical advances is easy to understand: The general public benefits from practitioners' mastery of improved surgical and diagnostic techiques. The successful translation of general scientific knowledge to specific medical techniques is one reason for American's growing life expectancy.

Other forms of technical education also are vital. The Technical Association of the Pulp & Paper Industry (TAPPI), Atlanta, an organization of nearly 30,000 members, conducts an extensive series of conferences and seminars, which represent the complex educational programs found in many trade associations. TAPPI divides itself into 11 technical divisions, including polymers, laminations and coatings, corrugated containers, engineering, environment, and research and development. A typical conference of the coating and graphics art division alone includes technical presentations, as well as a short course on a technical subject such as air knife coating, designed to "give professionals in line management, technical service, research and development, and the supplier industry an update on the 'hows' and 'whys' of air knife coating." Activities of this sort are part of the ongoing technical improvements that benefit the public by upgrading the product quality and reliability so often taken for granted.[5]

Leadership and Management Skills

Associations also offer an array of courses to members that present current trends in supervision, employee recognition, leadership, personnel, and financial management. The Healthcare Forum, San Francisco, for example, recently offered a three-day workshop for healthcare executives that focused on leadership, innovation, change, and systems thinking. Key conference faculty included leaders from the Massachusetts Institute of Technology and the University of Colorado. As with many association efforts, this session was approved for continuing education credit by relevant certifying bodies, in this case the American College of Physician Executives and the California Board of Registered Nursing.

The Hotel Sales and Marketing Association, Washington, D.C., offers workshops, workbooks, textbooks, and cassettes geared to management problems their members face: how to conduct market research, analyze marketing data, communicate effectively, and deal with specific market segments.

Improved leadership and management skills help the performance and careers of those members who attain them, as well as the public the association serves. Effective and vigorous leadership, sales and marketing attuned to customers, and coherent organizations are all likely to improve the utility of products and services delivered to customers.

Social Context

A third area of association education involves general questions of the context in which the association serves the larger world and the overall economy. Meetings and educational materials can be devoted to questions of ethics, responsibility, or an entire industry or service. The American Association of Museums, Washington, D.C., for example, devoted all 120 educational sessions at its 1988 convention to "exploring the idea that cultural and education institutions serve as catalysts to community economic development and growth."[6] TAPPI's environmental committee is an important mechanism through which industry members educate one another about "the effect of pulp paper and allied industry operations on the environment, particularly regarding air and water resources and solid waste disposal."[7]

Members of the Cosmetic, Toiletry and Fragrance Association (CFTA), Washington, D.C., "market the vast majority of all cosmetics, toiletries and fragrances sold in the United States," consisting of more than 18 billion products in 1988. A CFTA conference that same year considered worldwide cosmetic regulation, including regulatory practices and policies in Japan and the European Economic Community.

The San Francisco Medical Society, along with the Hastings Center, have created a quarterly educational forum for those who work in medical ethics. The meetings focus on substantive issues in medical ethics, operational tasks in managing ethics committees, and new areas meriting the development of guidelines.

These areas—technique, management, and social or political context—are the heart of association member educational efforts. By serving their members, associations serve a broader public as they enhance the quality of products and services available to consumers.

Technical improvements, better leadership and managerial skills, and enhanced competitive abilities within industries are elements central to effective private enterprise, professional development, and performance among nonprofits. One would have to question their very utility to seriously question the desirability of education as a way to improve them. Even in areas where industries are often challenged, for example, with regard to the physical environment, association education is a central way in which improvements can be transmitted and assessed. TAPPI's activities are a good example.

PUBLIC INFORMATION

The second major element of association education is that of educating or informing the public, which may be broken into three subsets: educating the public about general causes, services, or products, about a producer's specific products or activities, and about issues or concerns connected to but not the substance of the association's work.

Generic Information

Public education includes broad advertising campaigns that promote a product, such as beef or dairy foods, rather than a specific company. The Better Home Heat Council (BHHC), Wellesley Hills, Massachusetts, for example, has four chief goals: to promote oil heat, to enable unified action on legislation and regulation, to encourage high standards of service and conduct, and to disseminate useful information to members of the industry and the consuming public.[8]

In 1983, BHHC began an advertising campaign based on the professionalism of fuel oil dealers, which marketed dealers as a whole, not any particular firm. This advertising, like any, benefits the public to the degree that the product is worthwhile. From an economic viewpoint, this means only that consumers demand the product: If advertising brings to light a product that the public wants but has forgotten, or if it stimulates demand by speaking the truth about the product, then a public interest has been served.

Some information campaigns seek to inform the public about a cause or service whose merits are not doubted. Much of the work of the American Heart Association and the American Cancer Society, for example, is devoted to warning the public about health risks and symptoms and encouraging treatment, as is much activity of associations that address less well-known diseases.

One of 10 policies of the Water Pollution Control Federation, Alexandria, Virginia, concerns public information. "The public must be made fully aware of the consequences of water pollution and the costs of its control, including both the costs of construction of facilities and the cost of management, operation, and maintenance of facilities. Only in this way can the public be prepared to sponsor and support sound water pollution control measures."[9]

Targeted Information

"Much association education is designed to improve the delivery of products and services."

The second major element of public information is that of giving consumers targeted information about particular products and services. Here, the effort is not so much to promote an industry or cause as it is to help consumers understand a product in greater detail than normal experience or advertising can provide. The American Academy of Facial Plastic and Reconstructive Surgery distributes a series of pamphlets on various aspects of plastic surgery. The general pamphlet on facial plastic surgery is over 20 pages and serves to "familiarize" the prospective patient "with some basic facts" about plastic surgery. More specific brochures cover skin irregularities and postoperative care. These pamphlets explain clearly and directly what specific surgeries are designed to achieve, as well as the attending risks and procedures. They enhance individual physicians' own explanations of procedures, without their individually producing a pamphlet. The genesis of this material in the association also helps negate any misleading information from an individual practitioner.

The National Council of Jewish Women, New York, is currently engaged in a three-year project to increase the number and recognition of high-quality child care providers. One element of the project is "to define and disseminate effective volunteer-supported child care projects."[10] In a similar vein, many associations that work against drug abuse inform the public about the health hazards of individual drugs, as well as campaign against their use.

An interesting example of a public information effort that disseminates both specific and generic information is the multifaceted effort of the Chemical Manufacturers Association (CMA), Washington, D.C. CMA harbors no illusions about its industry's image among a populace broadly concerned about health, safety, and the environment. One program, the Community Awareness and Emergency Response Process, begun in 1985, is designed to inform communities about the chemicals manufactured and stored in local plants and to coordinate area-wide emergency planning and response. The program includes early warning systems for areas an accidental chemical release would cover, a joint effort with the American Trucking Association, Alexandria, Virginia, to increase the safety of equipment needed to transport hazardous materials, and general measures to increase public understanding of cooperative safety efforts undertaken by plants and surrounding communities. Emergency planning and response programs are active in industrial facilities in 47 states, including 123 in Texas, for example, and 104 in California.

While at least a partial answer to public concerns and tied closely to government, the CMA program is primarily an initiative to change public perception about the chemical industry and to deal with operational issues in preventing and coping with emergencies.

Other CMA programs also focus on public information: Chemtec helps callers respond to chemical incidents and emergencies, the Chemical Referral Center annually handles thousands of nonemergency calls seeking information about chemicals, and still other programs provide training videos and workshops. Each program provides a public service while favorably affecting public perception about the safety and openness of the chemical industry.

Broad Social Concerns

The third major purpose of association public education is to inform about issues or circumstances beyond the immediate market or relevant group of products. Here, associations may enter the public debate about general economic conditions or the specific economic segment in which members are experts. Such programs tend to emanate from associations that are themselves general, such as the National Association of Manufacturers. Among other numerous examples are the work of various scientific associations to call attention to the grave situation of technical education in the United States; the efforts of the Medic Alert Foundation International, Turlock, California, to prepare the public to receive better emergency medical treatment; and the work of the National Health Council, New York, to tell people how to embark on health careers. The public benefits to the degree that healthy and honest advocacy is useful in national policies. General reminders about the overall impact of health or safety regulations on economic performance, for example, are often timely and important.

WORKFORCE TRAINING

Association-based or -organized education can be extremely useful in meeting industry's need for a properly trained workforce. The same focus on general concepts and strategies used to meet the special needs of managers and professionals also can be used to help train entry level workers or workers moving to positions of increasing skill. While business firms do much of this by themselves, associations can be particularly useful in organizing training if their members are small firms or professional groups and if the associations can efficiently inform the entire industry about effective new practices in one company. Associations also have the opportunity to use and encourage innovative approaches in computer-assisted learning, competency evaluation, and individually paced instruction, because they and their members are free from the rigors of formal educational systems and do not attempt to achieve the accompanying broad goals of schooling.

"Association education can be extremely useful in meeting needs for a properly trained workforce."

Since 1951, the American Hotel and Motel Association, Washington, D.C., has managed an Educational Institute, "the world's largest developer of hospitality industry training materials." The materials include interactive software, seminars, manuals, and videotapes, which are revised regularly to reflect contemporary technology and management practices. They are available to executives, employees, and people who wish to enter the field.[11]

Another significant example again comes from TAP-PI, which has a training program devoted to problems, solutions, and new approaches relevant to industry trainers. One situation involved a firm that needed to train field service and installation personnel in combustion engineering. Systems engineers, consultants, and videotapes were too narrow, expensive, or uninteresting, so the company decided to use TAPPI's interactive videodisc, "Papermaking, the Process and the Products." The videodisc proved to be flexible, stimulating, and effective. Another videodisc produced by the TAPPI Learning Center focuses on the kraft pulping process and includes an interactive simulation in an actual paper mill setting. The manager of new material pulping and bleaching at Weyerhauser reports, "To get any closer to the real thing, you would have to be in the mill."[12]

Education for nonmembers is often an explicit goal of cause-related and advocacy organizations. The American Association of University Women, Washington, D.C., for example, awards $1.5 million per year for graduate education, international exchange, and community projects.

Worker education organized by trade, professional, and cause-related and advocacy associations loses none of its significance or social benefit because its goal is greater productivity for particular firms and economic sectors. On the contrary, the discipline of measurable economic utility will always be a central factor in making education relevant to work. The need is evident for continuing education in a world of work undergoing extraordinarily rapid technological change.

The questions one should ask about association education center on its ability to meet its challenges. Do associations deliver genuine quality? Do they clearly see the need for serious continuing training in new techniques? Can they and their members see the importance of filling in with continuing training where school systems lapse? These questions attest to the actual and potential value of association education to society. They are questions of quality that one asks of any serious endeavor, and they implicitly acknowledge the value of association education to the public.

ENDNOTES

1. Allan Bloom, *The Closing of the American Mind* (New York: Simon and Schuster, 1987).
2. William Johnston and Arnold Packer, *Workforce 2000* (Indianapolis: Hudson Institute, 1987).
3. Katherine Gruber, ed., *Encyclopedia of Associations* (Detroit: Gale Research Company, 1989).
4. Society of Nuclear Medicine, *Catalog of Educational Materials* (Oak Brook, IL: Society of Nuclear Medicine, 1989).
5. Technical Association of the Pulp and Paper Industry, *Coating Chronicle*, February 1989.
6. American Association of Museums, *Annual Report* (Washington, D.C.: AAM, 1988).
7. Technical Association of the Pulp and Paper Industry, *Opportunities* (Atlanta: TAPPI, no date).
8. Better Home Heat Council, *What It Is, What It Does for Me and Why I Support It* (Wellesley Hills, MA, no date).
9. Water Pollution Control Federation, "Bylaws," *Journal of the Water Pollution Control Federation* 60 no. 3 (1988).

10. National Council of Jewish Women, *Center for the Child* (New York: National Council of Jewish Women, Fall-Winter 1988).
11. For a fuller sense of the American Hotel and Motel Association, see its Strategic Plans, 1989 and 1990 (Washington, D.C.: American Hotel and Motel Association, 1988, 1990).
12. Technical Association of the Pulp and Paper Industry, *Newsletter of the Training and Development Subcommittee*, November 1988.

 # Performance and Safety Standards

KEY FINDINGS

- Associations' members spend more than $14.5 billion to meet performance and safety standards that associations have helped to develop.
- These standards serve the public interest by raising the quality of goods and services, by increasing the compatibility of products, and by focusing energy on innovation and improvement.
- Standards enable the flow of information to consumers that market activity alone would not sufficiently provide.
- Standard setting serves the common interests of producers and providers by ensuring a good reputation for, clear information about, and efficient use of their products and services. Serving these interests also serves those of consumers.
- Associations are extremely important in creating and disseminating standards, precisely because they represent interests common to entire industries, professions, and causes.
- The public benefits of standard setting outweigh the potential costs.

One of the most important, yet least visible, contributions that associations make to society is in the creation of standards for products and services. Standardization takes two major forms: (1) creating standards for performance and safety, and (2) regularizing and limiting products and services to ensure they work compatibly with each other.

Associations participate in standard setting in various ways. In some cases, the associations themselves help create standards. The American Chemical Society, Washington, D.C., for example, maintains standards for chemical reagents. In other cases, associations help foster the creation of standards by a more comprehensive standard-setting organization such as the American Society for Testing and Materials (ASTM). The two major comprehensive organizations that create and coordinate standards, ASTM and the American National Standards Institute (ANSI), Washington, D.C., are themselves nonprofit associations. ASTM, for example, has more than 30,000 dues-paying members.

The survey indicates that 39 percent of national associations spend funds on setting performance and safety standards and 8 percent on certifying them. Trade associations lead this activity, with 50 percent involved in standard setting. Even more significant from an economic standpoint, when the survey responses are weighted to represent the entire survey universe, associations estimate their members spend more than $14.5 billion a year to meet standards that associations have had a hand in developing. This amount is so large that were one to halve it, it would still represent an enormous enterprise.

The amount of volunteer time devoted to standard setting also is impressive. Almost 32 percent of associations use volunteers for this activity, and just under 10 million volunteer hours, valued at $100 million, are devoted to this function.

SETTING STANDARDS

To understand how and when product and service standards benefit the general public, it is necessary to

"One of the most important contributions associations make is creating standards."

examine the process, substance, and organizational structure of standard setting. The utility of standards has been recognized at least since the Industrial Revolution, and formal associations to set standards in America began to be formed near the turn of the century. In 1898, ASTM's forerunner was formed; in 1905, a committee to develop worldwide electrical engineering standards was developed; and in 1911, the American Society of Mechanical Engineers, Alexandria, Virginia, created a committee to form specifications for constructing steam boilers.

There now exist hundreds of groups that write standards, with the largest—ASTM—publishing more than 8,000 technical standards for products, ranging from metals, to petroleum, to plastics, to computers. The national coordinating group, ANSI, administers a procedure to recognize certain standards as "American National Standards" (nearly 9,000 standards bear this designation) and to promote their use.

The development approximately 10 years ago of safety standards for high chairs exemplifies a typical procedure involving a trade association working with ASTM. The Juvenile Product Manufacturers Association, Moorestown, New Jersey, saw a need to reduce high chair hazards by having ASTM develop a voluntary standard for manufacturers. An ASTM technical committee, which in this instance as in others comprised consumers, government representatives, retailers, and manufacturers, worked two years to create a safety specification based on study of the causes of high chair accidents. The standard covered strength, sufficient child restraints, suitable assembly, and the like. Since standards lose much effect if consumers cannot easily tell whether the product conforms, a program was developed to certify that the chairs comply with the ASTM standard, according to independent laboratory tests.

Standards also are useful in ensuring in advance that products will perform adequately and services will be delivered according to some observable or measurable specification. Performance standards allow consumers to compare products and services and to know before purchase that performance will be adequate. They also allow consumers, and producers, to focus on the variety of possibilities that might define adequate performance—for example, with air conditioners, the speed of cooling, versus the machine's durability, versus the system's efficiency, versus maximum cooling capability—and to choose the desired mixture.

This kind of specification in requirements is perhaps the most obvious kind of standard, but it is only one of many. Standard test methods may be formed to evaluate the qualities of materials and ingredients; standard practices may be created for installing equipment, for example; and standard terminologies, classifications, and guides for action may be developed.

THE NEED FOR STANDARDS

The utility of standards in advancing safety and quality, however, does not explain why producers are willing to adhere to standards nor why consumers need them in the first place. One must also consider why market competition is sometimes insufficient to create high enough quality and safety and why general standards, if necessary, are not all created or mandated by government.

Producers and service providers wish to secure a wide market for their products and services, respectively. An item that is shoddy or unsafe will eventually harm the entire market for that product because it is often difficult for consumers to distinguish in advance the relative reliability of different brands or the quality of different items under a single brand name. All Cadillac sales can be harmed by a single inferior model, and all American cars can be harmed by a single manufacturer's inferior models. If the item is not absolutely necessary, substitutes will be sought, or, if the product is vital, government may be asked to step in. The general interest of producers and providers, however, is to expand the market for their products and services without undue interference. A firm may benefit in the near term from unsafe or shoddy goods, but in the long term the entire market for the product may be affected adversely. Creating general standards is, therefore, often in the interest of producers, especially those with a significant share of the market and long-term interests to protect. In this sense, product standards and many professional and ethical standards share the same function.

The interest of consumers in standards stems from the inability to have perfect information about many qualities of the goods and services they buy. Indeed, in some cases, this inherent lack of information may cause dangerous results out of all proportion to what a consumer would knowingly risk. The high chair example illustrates both points. Durability and strength are somewhat, but not completely, visible, and the consequences of failure are enormous. Similarly, automobiles have hundreds of parts that consumers know almost nothing about.

The effect of low quality should eventually be to eliminate poor products and services from the market, but at what cost before a poor reputation is recognized? Because the cause of a poor product or service may take too long to be visible or because the results of waiting may be too costly to health or safety, the market alone cannot always force high standards in a timely and effective way. Some set of commonly adhered to standards serves to alleviate consumers' inevitable ignorance about many qualities.

Government may take the market's place and mandate standards. But standards created by an association of private producers, perhaps with government, academic, and consumer participation, are generally to be preferred. Associations are flexible and adaptable in a way that government is not; they place responsibility where it belongs—in the hands of producers and consumers; they keep the formulation of standards close to the technical expertise on which they draw.

THE COSTS OF STANDARDS

There are, of course, costs to standards. Meeting standards makes goods and services more expensive. This is obvious with products, such as lawnmowers or automobiles, that must be redesigned or incorporate new materials to meet safety requirements. Cost is also a factor even when major redesign is not necessary to meet standards. When standards broadly apply to an entire product line, moreover, they often take away the consumer's choice to pay less and receive less. They may even cause goods with certain qualities to temporarily leave the market. Consider the difficulty in purchasing a high-performance automobile at a reasonable price from 1975 to 1985.

Moreover, meeting performance or safety standards may conceivably restrict innovation by forcing products into narrowly defined molds or by restricting efficient production combinations of, say, safety and speed or safety and beauty. Occasionally, standards can have the effect of driving underfunded or threatening innovative competitors from the market.

Such serious questions do not negate the general utility of standards; rather, they point to a lack of

"Association-created standards are generally to be preferred to government regulation."

clarity about the effect that excessively rigorous requirements, overly generous liability awards, and the like may have on the technical innovation that is key to performance, reliability and, safety. Yet, these are cautions, rather than reasons to bemoan all standards. Some argue that standards increase competition by allowing new firms to make parts and products that are interchangeable with more established items. Furthermore, as mentioned previously, consumers lack sufficient information to choose intelligently in every instance. They have made it clear in recent years that they wish producers and service providers to adhere to higher and higher levels of quality and safety. They have also made clear their willingness to absorb many of the costs.

That standards are on the whole desirable does not mean associations always welcome them. On the contrary, they sometimes oppose government or international standards that limit or restrict excessively. One would hardly expect an industry to take steps to increase its costs if it sees no benefits to reap or visible dangers to eliminate. In this sense, government at its best will always be necessary to speak for the public interest.

In practice, however, government often is guided by the most vocal or powerful private interests, and various interlocking government regulations and restrictions will often be unintentionally stifling. The effect may be to limit innovation or narrow the range of available products and services more than consumers would desire in the long run. Consequently, private self-regulation that formulates and adopts general standards where market forces do not suffice is often better tailored to meet general needs than the government.

Performance and safety standards, then, benefit the general public by helping to ensure quality and safety where consumers lack information. The trick is to set standards in a way that does not unintentionally stifle competition or retard technological development. Standards set or encouraged by associations are a useful way to accomplish this goal. Standards that are privately and voluntarily created and met in a system which encourages appropriate government participation are perhaps the best way to bring about quality and safety, with a minimum of rigidity.

A more specific discussion of procedures and examples will provide a better sense of associations' role in standard setting, of the public utility of standards, and of the enormous scope of the standard-setting activity.

PUBLIC-PRIVATE COOPERATION

ASTM had nearly 140 technical committees at the beginning of 1989, grouped according to the following subject areas: ferrous metals, nonferrous metals, ceramic and concrete materials, miscellaneous materials, materials for specific applications, deterioration of materials, and miscellaneous subjects. Within these categories, subcommittees consider standards for a host of areas, including, for example, metallic-coated iron and steel, magnetic properties, electrical conductors, metallic materials for thermostats, cement, concrete pipe, advanced ceramics, paint, wood, rubber, roofing, soaps, engine coolants, leather, catalysts, and waste disposal. They further consider fire standards, nuclear technology, quality and statistically computerized systems, and coolants. They also look at materials in specific products: electronics, surgical materials, floor covering, sports equipment, tires, amusement rides, and search and rescue. This list only scratches the surface: It is fair to say that no significant area of American industry is left untouched by ASTM standards.

"There now exist hundreds of groups that write standards."

ASTM standards committees comprise members of industry, government, trade associations, and the general public, the latter often represented by academics who understand the technical issue at hand. The U.S. Commerce Department's National Bureau of Standards and Technology provides hundreds of staff members to serve on ASTM technical committees, and its director sits on the ASTM and ANSI boards. Members of other government agencies also serve on the committees. The result is close cooperation among government, industry, and associations in what is basically a voluntary nongovernment enterprise. (This cooperation was encouraged as a matter of government policy in a 1982 Office of Management and Budget [OMB] circular.) All technical committee members serve voluntarily, and unless government mandates a standard, adherence is also voluntary.

Government support for associations' role in setting standards was enunciated clearly by Douglas Ginsburg when he administered regulatory affairs at OMB: "In examining the alternatives for addressing a problem, one alternative we hold up against the [government] agencies' proposals is industry self-regulation. In areas like these, [there is] a rebuttable presumption in order to justify a federal regulatory program in these areas."[1]

This OMB support is all the more significant because it is mindful of the possible difficulties. Wrote Ginsburg,

"We encourage industry-wide cooperation in determining product standards for items that are of the greatest benefit when they are interchangeable. We encourage the development and dissemination of criteria that help consumers evaluate services that are complex, or may require a professional education to provide. But we oppose any unnecessary restrictions on entry...[and] favor performance standards over design standards."[2]

As James Miller put it when he headed the Federal Trade Commission, "I'm a strong supporter of industry self-regulation. The vast majority of commercial transactions work well, without need for interference of any kind. In some cases, however, the market 'fails,' and regulation of some kind is warranted. But this need not be government regulation if industry self-regulation is superior."[3]

A sophisticated level of public-private cooperation also helps to control possible unfairness. ASTM committees, for example, first use task forces to draft standards. Subcommittee members vote on these draft standards, followed by the full committee, and then the entire association. Balloting is by mail, and substantial revisions are voted on once again. Revisions are based on negative votes and their accompanying explanations; persuasive negatives have led to changes in almost all originally drafted standards. Once the vote is concluded, a committee on standards conducts a review to make certain that proper procedures have been followed; this group also serves as the appeals board. Only after this entire process is a proposal adopted as an official ASTM standard.[4]

ASTM follows several other procedures to help ensure that due process is followed, no restraint of trade exists, and standards are promulgated by responsible authorities. There is timely notice to affected parties, for example, and wide opportunity to participate in decisions. As ASTM writes, "In order for standards to avoid restraint of trade...measures must be taken to prevent them from unreasonably restricting competition by stifling innovation or by excluding potential competitors from established markets. Care must be taken to assure that the interest of those who consume materials and products are not sacrificed to the interests of those who produce them."[5] This result is effected by making certain (1) that producers are not committee chairs; (2) that on certain committees, user, consumer, and general interest voters equal or outweigh producer voters; (3) that meetings are open; and (4) that standards are reviewed every five years.

SAFETY STANDARDS

The complexity of these procedures gives some sense of the efforts taken to ensure a fair process, and the list of committees gives some sense of the scope. One also needs to consider how requests for standards originate, and what the role is for associations other than those like ASTM whose central purpose involves standards. As indicated earlier, associations often initiate a request for a standard. In 1989, for example, the National School Supply and Equipment Association, Arlington, Virginia, requested consideration of safety standards for public playground equipment. These standards are being considered under several rubrics, including installation, maintenance, and falls.

To take another example, more than 10 years ago the American Recreational Equipment Association (AREA), Delaware, Ohio, asked ASTM to develop standards for maintaining and safely operating amusement park rides. The committee selected to formulate the standards grew out of wide-ranging discussions in which several trade associations participated, among them, the Outdoor Amusement Business Association, Minneapolis; the International Association of Amusement Parks and Attractions, Alexandria, Virginia; and AREA. These groups, in turn, stimulated ride manufacturers, amusement park operators, and the government to participate. Associations were the focal point for attracting broad involvement and for working through the differing economic interests of their members.

The Cosmetic, Fragrance and Toiletry Association (CFTA), conducts a program of ingredient review through its Cosmetic Ingredient Review (CIR) group. CIR's purpose is to "review and document the safety of ingredients used in cosmetic products."

CIR staff gather all existing data on nearly 3,000 ingredients. A panel of toxicologists, pharmacologists, and other scientists then judges the data, using procedures similar to those of the U.S. Food and Drug Administration (FDA). The forum is open to the public, and consumer, industry, and government personnel serve as nonvoting members. The panels' decisions are subjected to peer review and published. Data are made available to FDA and other government agencies. Much of the data are submitted voluntarily by CFTA members. This self-conducted safety screening has until recently preempted congressional legislation.[6] While it does not issue standards per se, CIR represents an important example of industry self-regulation conducted through an association.

Another example of association-based standard setting may be seen in the work of the Association of Home Appliance Manufactures (AHAM), Chicago. As Michael Hunt has written, AHAM's experience at least partially contradicts the "conventional wisdom among economists," which argues that trade associations are powerless in unconcentrated industries and redundant in concentrated ones.

AHAM has worked with Underwriters Laboratories, Northbrook, Illinois, to develop minimum safety standards for aspects of home appliances, such as wiring. Such standards, Hunt argues, may reduce legal action against manufacturers, increase overall demand (especially for brands with several products), and theoretically, in some instances, serve as barriers to entering the marketplace. Standards also help to discourage government intervention. Hunt also notes that such safety standards help consumers in the many instances where they cannot intelligently purchase as much or as little safety as they want and no single firm can profitably supply the necessary facts.[7]

"Performance standards allow consumers to compare products along a number of dimensions."

PERFORMANCE STANDARDS

AHAM also has developed product standards specifying performance in terms of purpose and function, for example, how much dirt a washer removes from clothes. Such standards go beyond safety minimums. Product standards developed by AHAM are then certified by ANSI.

Performance standards are especially important because they enable one to measure such variables as speed, reliability, cleanliness, and cooling under a variety of conditions and to evaluate a product's salient features. They also enable consumers to compare the products of various manufacturers along a number of dimensions. In addition, they focus manufacturers' changes and improvements on specific areas and place advertising claims within a context of reasonable comparison. They preempt government standards if they take into account characteristics of product performance, such as pollution, that are important to government or the public.

Performance and safety standards constitute the most visible and perhaps the most significant area of standardization. Associations are especially important in this process because voluntary agreement to abide by standards works best with, and sometimes even requires, the members' unanimity. Attaining this type of agreement requires an independent staff to make suitable decisions that would be too costly and difficult were each separate player expected to independently negotiate. Moreover, associations often have information and expertise that government does not, making associations' self-regulation less costly.

While most of the examples cited in this chapter involve trade associations, professional societies and cause-related and advocacy groups also are involved in setting standards. The American Dental Association (ADA), Chicago, for example, certifies the safety and effectiveness of materials used by dentists, as well as of rinses, toothbrushes, and other products used at home. Products that meet ADA standards after examination and review can display the ADA seal of certification. The American Red Cross, Washington, D.C., develops and maintains standards for testing, handling, and evaluating the safety of blood products. The Joint Commission on Accreditation of Health Care Organizations, Chicago, develops standards for the operation of hospitals and regularly conducts site inspections. The American Diabetes Association, Alexandria, Virginia, maintains standards for health care providers in their role as educators of diabetics and conducts periodic reviews of these education programs.

STANDARDS FOR COMPATIBILITY AND INTERCHANGEABILITY

Another major form of standards addresses the compatibility and interchangeability of products and parts of different manufacturers by limiting dimensions and variety. The classic examples are the standardization of brick sizes after the Boston fire of 1689; of railroad track gauge, legally mandated in 1863; and of interchangeable parts for simplified musket production pioneered by Eli Whitney. The first two examples involved government action, indicating that voluntary compliance with standards is sometimes impractical or impossible.

Compatibility standards generally differ from performance and safety standards because their purpose is to allow goods to be efficiently used in tandem and parts to be regularized across manufacturers, as opposed to setting and measuring the characteristics of materials or finished goods.

These distinctions among the types of standards are not hard and fast. ASTM, for example, maintains specifications for structural steel that denominate thickness, strength, and composition. To be considered structural steel, the product must contain the specified characteristics. The effect of these specifications not only allows comparison between the quality of products, but also allows better integration of construction at different sites and eliminates unnecessary grades. Local building codes adopt many association standards in order to help assure quality and safety and to allow interchangeability.

One interesting example of the comparability process exists in the farm machinery industry. Firms have both incentives and disincentives for promoting interchangeability, centering around the degree to which product lines of particular producers are complete, are tied together, and are distributed through exclusive retail outlets. The Society of Automotive Engineers (SAE) and the American Society of Agricultural Engineers (ASAE), St. Joseph, Michigan, have jointly developed a variety of standards for farm machinery, but the degree of adoption has varied across the industry.

"Product compatibility may benefit producers and consumers in different ways."

On the one hand, standardization would enable farm machinery suppliers other than major producers to produce parts more profitably, and the availability of spare parts would make it sensible for farmers to risk purchasing machines from new producers. For these very reasons, however, individual firms, especially large ones, sometimes find that adhering to cross-industry standards is not useful. The perspective on and resolution of the issue revolve around the way in which firms perceive the pace and source of innovation (which will sometimes lead producers to want industry-wide standards in order to benefit from new techniques) and the stability of their market shares.

The point is that compatibility may benefit producers and consumers in different ways: Standardization is sometimes in producers' interests and sometimes not. The entire history of standards in the computer industry, as opposed to proprietary activity, is another example of this sort of economic complexity. Generally, voluntary adherence to standards increasingly is seen to make economic sense in this highly competitive domestic and international market.

It is important to recognize the role of SAE and ASAE in creating the farm machinery standards and making them available to be adhered to when business or political incentives are present. From the professional viewpoint, reducing variety in components that do not differ functionally increases availability and decreases cost. Furthermore, as Robert Kudrle indicates, choosing compatibility standards—such as the distance between bolt holes on a wheel—does not reduce technical innovation. From this perspective, standardization is "socially beneficial."[8]

Indeed, as former FTC and OMB Chairman James Miller said, "Certification permits manufacturers to demonstrate efficiently that their products comply with relevant standards. One obvious benefit of these programs is to facilitate the introduction of new technology by enabling innovative manufacturers to demonstrate the safety or efficiency of new products. More generally, standards and certification programs facilitate communication between buyers and sellers about complex product attributes."[9]

It is also important to realize that product and service specifications exist where one does not usually think to look for them. ADA, for example, working through ANSI, helps to develop specifications for orthodontic bands, amalgams for fillings, and other manufactured products. These standards are the benchmark against which products are measured and certified.

The benefits to the general public from association efforts in making or suggesting standards are, in general, substantial. At their best, performance, safety, and compatibility standards help define the area where producers' and providers' general concerns intersect with consumers' general concerns within the same market. Within this overlapping realm, associations' service to their members' collective interests emerges as service to the general public, which seeks quality, safety, and efficiency. Standards fill information gaps that individuals will always confront in a complex, technologically based economy filled with many interrelated intermediate and final products. According to ASTM, standards enhance the ability "to purchase, manufacture, and distribute more easily and cheaply." They increase consumers' confidence in what they purchase and how to use it. They lower producers' inventories and improve quality control and performance. Fair standards, then, help both consumers and producers. They are not a product of altruism, but arise from the mutual interests of buyers and sellers.

This is not to suggest that every effort to standardize is unproblematic, for standard setting involves economic motives of individual producers and providers who are concerned with their own share of relevant markets.

Association-controlled performance, safety, and compatibility standards can sometimes limit innovation or create difficult barriers to entry. Government standards and regulations, however, often produce the same effect, especially when the concern with safety exceeds that of producers or the general public. Government's distance from the responsibilities of producing and selling profitably always threatens to separate its actions from the discipline of markets.

In general, voluntary standards created after broad participation are to be preferred. Indeed, government would serve the public interest as much by controlling whatever economic harm may arise from inappropriate standards as by mandating restrictions that go beyond sensible economic calculations. On the whole, self-regulatory efforts, resulting in standards formulated with significant association participation, are a genuine public benefit that deserves greater recognition.

ENDNOTES

1. Douglas H. Ginsburg, "Administration Efforts to Enhance the Opportunities for Self-Regulation," in *Proceedings of the White House Conference on Self Regulation* (Washington, D.C.: American Society of Association Executives, 1984), 18.
2. Ibid.
3. James Miller III, "Maximizing the Benefits of Self-Regulation," in *Proceedings*, 6.
4. American Society for Testing and Materials, 20 *Questions about ASTM* (Philadelphia: ASTM, no date).
5. Ibid.
6. Cosmetic, Toiletry and Fragrance Association, *CIR Developments*, January 12, 1989.
7. Michael Hunt, "Trade Associations and Self-Regulation: Major Home Appliances," in *Regulating the Product*, ed. Richard E. Caves and Marc J. Roberts (Cambridge: Ballinger, 1975), 39-55.
8. Robert T. Kudrle, "Regulation and Self-Regulation in the Farm Machinery Industry," in *Regulating the Product*, 57-73.
9. Miller, *Proceedings*, 7.

 # Codes of Ethics and Professional Standards

KEY FINDINGS

- ☐ Codes of ethics and professional standards serve the public by increasing trust in professionials' integrity and competence—qualities not easily judged before purchase.
- ☐ Codes of ethics focus professionals' and producers' attention on practices that support a healthy market which are not always guaranteed by individual activities.
- ☐ Codes of ethics offer added public value by providing an occasion for thoughtful deliberation, thereby increasing professional and business responsibility.
- ☐ Issues that merit continued discussion include the questions sometimes raised about the appropriateness of legally mandated licensing in some occupations and about the questionable limits on behavior (for example, advertising) endorsed in some codes of ethics. Such concerns do not obviate the utility of private self-regulation in helping to ensure trust in the skills and integrity of professionals and producers, for this trust serves both the collective interest of association members and the general public interest.

Questions of professional and business ethics are increasingly visible. Journalists who record politicians' possible conflicts of interest, for example, cannot avoid asking and being asked about their own ethical standing. Should they accept speaking or consulting fees from the government? Should they receive pay from controversial private groups? Should they reveal the sources of their honoraria?

Newspapers and television networks set many rules and judgments individually. *The Washington Post*, for example, recently ordered a reporter to decline a fee from a political group associated with Unification Church head Sun Myung Moon.[1]

Often, however, rules are determined collectively. The press group that administers credentials for journalists who cover Congress engaged in a lengthy debate in 1988 and 1989 about reporting and accepting honoraria. The debate culminated in the election of officers who represented those arguing against stringent prohibitions.

Physicians and attorneys traditionally have set standards for ethical practice. These standards are subject to growing scrutiny and analysis. The complexity of medical practice; the increasing possibilities for prolonging life when consciousness has been lost; and the difficult issues of the cost and availability of drugs, organ transplants, and other care force medical ethics to be discussed explicitly and comprehensively. For many large law firms the desire to grow and expand, to merge, and to fight mergers has become dominant. Lawyers' behavior often appears to be governed as much by business choice as by professional necessity. Questions unavoidably are asked about the place of *pro bono* work, about the legal as opposed to financial justification for litigation, and about competition for clients.

In law and medicine, the chief venues for prudently considering ethical issues are the American Medical Association (AMA), Chicago, and the American Bar Association (ABA), Chicago, and their state and local counterparts. Indeed, professional and trade associations are central in collectively thinking through standards that govern ethical behavior within the many occupations they represent.

Many associations help set codes of ethics. The survey results revealed that 31 percent of associations tie some budget expenditure to setting codes of ethics and 17 percent help to enforce them. Of professional associations, 39 percent help set ethical standards and 21 percent help to enforce them. For cause-related and advocacy associations the numbers are roughly 15 percent for both functions, and for trade associations, 27 percent and 13 percent, respectively.

These percentages somewhat understate the total association effort. For example, volunteers devote some time to setting codes of ethics within more than 34 percent of professional associations and 26 percent of trade associations.

While the proportion of associations involved in ethical standards is obviously large, it falls below the number that spend resources on conventions (90 percent), education (89 percent), public information (71 percent), and research (64 percent). It is closest in magnitude to the percentage of associations involved in setting product standards (31 percent), setting professional standards (24 percent), and providing community service (20 percent).

The associations surveyed spent approximately 1 percent of their total annual dollar expenditures—roughly $71 million—on this function. This is still a significant sum, though well below the $785 million spent on community service, for example. Helping to set and enforce codes of ethics, then, is a significant but not overwhelming part of association activity.

THE BENEFITS OF ETHICAL STANDARDS
Enhancing Trust

What use to the general public are ethical canons? First, they help to raise trust in products and producers where individual consumers lack knowledge and cannot make fully informed judgments. Consumers often must choose professional practitioners and courses of action without fully understanding the grounds for choice. The heart of a genuine profession is its basis in special training, which is unfamiliar to consumers and not easily understood. A consumer can often judge results—was the case won or the illness cured—but does not know what methods are commonly accepted or likely to work. This gives professionals and individual providers easy opportunities for fraud. Therefore, part of professionalism involves codes of behavior that control such possibilities by setting standards of activity and skill, which heighten consumers' security. Indeed, professionals usually regard themselves as different from businesspeople primarily because their actions are governed by a notion of appropriate service, behavior, and technique.

Professional associations are a natural venue in which to shape codes of ethics. Medical and bar associations often have extremely complex codes, sometimes backed by enforcement procedures tied to legal sanctions. These codes are distributed widely and help to form the ethos guiding practitioners' activities.

The San Francisco Medical Society, for example, publishes AMA's "Principles of Medical Ethics" in its new member handbook.[2] The handbook includes the most important interpretations of these principles from *The Current Opinions of the Judicial Council of the American Medical Association.* The second principle addresses honesty and trust: "A physician shall deal honestly with patients and colleagues and strive to expose those physicians deficient in character or competence, or who engage in fraud or deception."[3] The principle recognizes physicians' responsibility to police their own conduct and that of their peers, implicitly indicating the opportunities for deception existing within the profession.

The use of codes to enhance consumer trust is not limited to professional organizations. There are many other areas where buyers tend to distrust sellers because a product is amorphous, complex, or delivered well after payment, if ever. To moderate consumer distrust and enhance goodwill, it is often useful to adopt elements of professionalism from the learned professions.

There may or may not be a "science" to public relations, but guidelines for behavior make sense. The Public Relations Society of America (PRSA), New York, has had a code of professional standards since 1950. Included are elements advocating high standards of honestly and integrity, fair dealing, not guaranteeing the achievement of specified results beyond the members' control, "not representing conflicting or competing interests," and not disseminating false information.[4]

The National Association of Mutual Insurance Agents, Alexandria, Virginia, to take a related example, has adopted a one-page code of ethics, most of which is a series of pledges to the public. Among the pledges are the following:

I will thoroughly analyze the insurance needs of my clients and recommend the forms of indemnity best suited to those needs, regardless of the measure of profit to myself.

I regard the insurance business as an honorable profession, rather than as a mere business.[5]

Professionalism in the sense of serving the public interest is an important way in which practitioners clarify a profession's validity beyond merely amassing profits. Associations are a central vehicle for generating this sense and for organizing the codes, meetings, and discussions that help to bring this sense to life.

Raising Awareness

A second way in which codes of ethics serve the public is by focusing attention on concerns that pure market considerations might overlook or ignore. In one sense, consumers are served efficiently when the product or service is sold for the cheapest price. As previously suggested, however, consumers cannot always easily know how much of a service to purchase to get a job done or the qualitative differences between apparently identical products. It is, therefore, useful to have informal mechanisms to enhance consumers' confidence that they are not buying too much of an unnecessary good. Ethical codes are one such mechanism, offered from the practitioner's side. They are useful in creating trust because they force the seller to confront practices that constitute selling too much of a useless or harmful thing. They also lead the seller to attend to practices that generally support fair markets, even if these practices are ignored in any particular transaction. They help support modes of behavior that are desirable apart from their economic meaning.

PRSA, for example, enjoins its members from accepting fees from anyone except clients or employers without consent and from engaging "in any practice which has the purpose of corrupting the integrity of the channels of communications or the processes of government." More positively, "a member shall conduct his or her professional life in accord with the public interest."[6] Codes of ethics focus attention on motives beyond the market (the public interest), on practices that harm markets (corrupting government process), and on practices that distort particular transactions (working covertly for two

"Consumers cannot always know how much of a service to purchase or the differences between apparently identical products."

masters). Ethical codes and the associations that organize them serve the public interest in identifying both harmful practices and broad positive motives.

Encouraging Reflection

Codes of ethics have a third function, that of providing occasion for deliberation about ethical issues. One might say that codes of ethics merely reflect common standards of decent behavior and are, therefore, unnecessary. But formulating, interpreting, and considering codes enable association members to deliberately consider general injunctions and to be constantly reminded of their importance. They also force reflection on the order of importance of various standards and their meaning and applicability in the business or profession.

Such deliberation focuses thought and attention and enhances responsibility. It stimulates attention to ethical matters in a way that general injunctions not specific to the activity or injunctions delivered by others cannot.

The role of associations is especially important here, because associations are forums in which these deliberations take place. Associations offer opportunities for organized discussion throughout the membership when codes are reformulated and interpreted, along with the serious authority of peer endorsement when first considered and adopted.

The opportunity for serious reasoned reflection is enhanced when codes of ethics are regularly updated, interpreted, or enforced. AMA's code, for example, is constantly updated through *The Current Opinions* of its Judicial Council. Bar association codes also are reviewed frequently. PRSA revised its codes in 1954, 1959, 1963, 1977, 1983, and 1988.

Preempting Government

When fostering ethical practices and deliberations, codes of conduct presumably also affect members' behavior in other spheres—a fourth social benefit. A fifth and final benefit is that of filling a vacuum or preempting government. Without association-generated codes, it is hard to envision how professional or industry canons would otherwise spontaneously arise. The need for or wish to have a code is one way in which an activity groups itself. Associations are key to defining and setting directions for their groups. Were codes not to arise through associations, they and related activities might be mandated by government.

There are two main reasons why government-devised or -mandated codes are less desirable than voluntarily generated association codes. First, this society prefers citizens to do their own work. Taking responsibility for one's actions and deliberately applying one's talent in a common effort should not be left to government alone. It is much more in accord with individual freedom and the exercise of individual rights to form and manage one's own common enterprise than to leave these functions to government. This is true even if the finished product is inferior to what government might have constructed.

Second, those closest to an occupation or event usually understand nuances and expectations better than government, which will always be somewhat remote. Lawmakers recognize this fact when they conduct hearings and investigations before writing legislation affecting constituents.

Third, government action carries the threat and reality of punishment. It is bulky and obtrusive. It tends to diminish risk and innovation and to increase bureaucracy and administration. Government-mandated codes and procedures, in fact, sometimes favor the elements in an occupation least open to competition and change. (There are instances, of course, in which government action may be necessary to meet a need not otherwise being met, and legal and regulatory proceedings may favor innovation. The court cases dealing with advertising fees and competition among physicians and lawyers are cases in point.) And, when codes of ethics, such as those of physicians and lawyers, have legal or quasi-legal status, they are more apt to mistake the interests of professionals for the interests of the entire profession or community.

From this perspective, the National Recovery Administration (NRA) in the 1930s was a wholesale experiment in government codes often dominated by industry associations, with unhappy and, ultimately, unconstitutional results. As Lewis Galambos writes:

> Between March, 1935, and the spring of 1937, the Cotton-Textile Institute [CTI] and American public policy on business both experienced a series of significant changes. In May, 1935, the National Industrial Recovery Act [NIRA] was declared unconstitutional by the Supreme Court. Suddenly and swiftly CTI fell from the position of power that it occupied when

"Those closest to an occupation or event usually understand nuances and expectations better than government."

the recovery administration granted to the association leaders a limited prerogative to control the production of cotton goods.

With the demise of the NRA, the alliance between the trade associations and the government reverted to its earlier, pre-New Deal form. The associations, including CTI, continued to cooperate with the federal government; in a wide variety of activities the trade organizations and the government still shared the same goals. But public policy on competition slipped back into its traditional American stance.

This shift in public policy had an important effect upon the trade association movement in cotton textiles. The associations did not wither away. But insofar as a movement involves a series of interrelated organizational and ideological changes which advance along a certain course, toward a certain objective, the trade association movement was interrupted by the death of the NRA.[7]

Government-mandated ethical codes fall far short of the NRA's government-association mandated wage and production controls. Still, they indicate the potential harm of government control over industries and professions or of nongovernmental association codes with both legal authority and a tendency to restrict competition. Perhaps the best way for association codes of conduct to serve their functions without inappropriately restricting markets is for them to shy from incorporating strictly economic judgments of individual members. Such restrictions, of course, are no better when practiced by government.

Those who construct codes are most effective when they focus on competence, fair dealing, honesty, and a sense of service, and not on immediate economic issues. The goal of successful codes is to enhance the health and trustworthiness of an entire profession or industry and the health of common market conditions which support those individual economic decisions necessary for practice.

Limited in this way, codes of ethics will normally preempt direct government efforts. The benefit is the responsibility, subtlety, and potentially greater openness and market fairness discussed. Problems of enforcement are not sufficient reason to turn to government, except with difficulties with public safety and health. Clear statements of culpability, with proper procedural safeguards, are sufficient warning to consumers about a professional's reputation.

ONE ASSOCIATION'S EXPERIENCE

An additional example of an extensive ethics program, which illuminates the overall purpose, utility, and operation of codes of ethics is that formulated by the Direct Selling Association (DSA), Washington, D.C. DSA's members sell products door to door or through home parties. Approximately 10 years ago, DSA, which comprises roughly 100 firms accounting for 70 percent of total industry sales, decided to reverse the industry's reputation as one that often used deceptive practices to one oriented to consumer protection. A key element of this plan was to develop and enforce a code of behavior. According to DSA President Neil Offen, "The seed for developing an effective self-regulatory mechanism was planted out of economic necessity and the desire of industry leaders to counter a negative image and speak out on behalf of a method of retailing that provided all Americans income opportunities and consumer quality products and services at fair prices."[8]

Developing a code with teeth was especially difficult in direct selling because of the more than five million people through whom direct selling firms work. Nonetheless, the large industry leaders supported the code.

The code is essentially a consumer protection code whose effect is to "make restitution to consumers who have been mistreated and, thereby, make it more difficult for charlatans to deceive the public." The code establishes "ethical principles and practices" concerning guarantees, terms of sale, truthfulness, and the responsibility of companies for their salespersons' and distributors' actions.[9] This last provision is central to making the code genuinely operational, as is DSA's establishing a mechanism for enforcement that relies on an independent code administrator. Participating companies have over the past 10 years remedied each complaint the administrator has declared valid, partially because he has authority to refer complaints for legal action.

The information campaign to publicize the code and to campaign against unscrupulous practices (such as pyramid schemes where rights are sold to sell products to others, instead of products themselves) has increased the industry's overall reliability.

The code cannot be enforced against nonmembers, however, and the association's legal and legislative benefits may not be enough to attract new members in the absence of accreditation and product marketing services. Direct selling is an activity marked by great ease of entry; it is a

"Codes of ethics help consumers overcome inadequate information."

major source of part-time work and second incomes. The industry and the association, therefore, oppose occupational licensing, arguing that the code fosters competition by improving general market conditions for legitimate merchants, rather than by limiting entry. Those who created the DSA code have been extremely sensitive to the possible antitrust implications inherent in any code and, accordingly, have instituted strict procedures and conducted discussions with Federal Trade Commission officials to counteract these possibilities.

The effect of these restrictions is to make strict enforcement impossible. But the participation of major sellers and general promotion of legitimate practice still benefit consumers and major sellers, even making it reasonable for major sellers to consider mechanisms to aid consumers with sound complaints against nonmembers.

Ethical codes help consumers overcome inadequate information about many products and procedures, particularly those of professionals. They focus attention on conditions necessary for the general health of a profession or industry and society as a whole. They foster reflection and deliberation, leading those who formulate or consider codes to take responsibility for a community larger than themselves in an informed way. They, thus, help foster attributes central to a liberal democracy. To the degree that associations are an important arena for codes of ethics and their members reach beyond their potential for self-interest, codes of ethics are a significant service to society.

PROFESSIONAL STANDARDS

Associations also help to set and enforce professional standards. Although the distinction between these standards and codes of ethics is not clear-cut, professional standards generally go beyond ethics in that they attempt to cover professional conduct in general and not solely questions of morality. Professional standards, especially in tandem with certification programs, concern the entire scope of professional competence.

Nearly 24 percent of the associations surveyed set professional standards and 15 percent certify that these standards have been met. More professional than other types of associations set these standards, but they are joined by nearly 20 percent of trade associations.

Professional standards benefit the public by giving some assurance that the professionals consumers employ have reflected thoughtfully about their practices. They also help mitigate consumers' uncertainty about the skills of those they are considering hiring, as discussed earlier. A third benefit to the public is that of helping to ensure that people with identical titles deliver roughly similar services.

Technical Occupations

Several significant examples of professional standards exist. The Council of Engineering and Scientific Society Executives (CESSE), Washington, D.C., which represents executives from 150 scientific and engineering societies, supports many member-managed accreditation and certification programs. According to CESSE, these "enhance the public health, safety and welfare at no cost to government by insuring that individuals wishing to practice in a scientific or engineering field meet certain standards of competence."[10]

The American Association of Cost Engineers, Morgantown, West Virginia, tests credentials of candidates who wish to attain "Certified Cost Engineer" status. The American Concrete Institute, Detroit, certifies people who test, inspect, and work with concrete. The Institute of Industrial Engineers, Norcross, Georgia, will soon begin to certify industrial engineers in specialty areas such as systems integration.

Scientific and engineering societies also accredit university programs and other training programs; the link between professional standards and education is obviously close. The American Chemical Society includes chemistry departments that adhere to its guidelines on college curricula appropriate for obtaining degrees, and the American Society of Mechanical Engineers supports accreditation of mechanical engineering and technology programs.

A central purpose of bar, medical, engineering, and accounting associations is to help develop and enforce professional standards. Clearly, the heart of professional expertise is found first in undergraduate and graduate training and in state licensing procedures. But major professional associations participate through peer review, organizing courses that meet continuing education requirements, and creating and enforcing standards that can form the basis for legal disciplinary action.

The professional standards of the American Institute of Certified Public Accountants (AICPS), New York, is an especially significant document. It covers many ethical issues but also deals with competence. Violations of the standards are subject to disciplinary actions, ranging from reprimand, to expulsion from the national or state society, to suspension or withdrawal of one's license to practice. Losing membership in a state CPA society is harmful, indeed, to any accountant, and the willingness of state societies to police the code by referring serious violators to state licensing boards gives the association special power. Moreover, the designation of Certified Public Accountant is awarded only after a rigorous qualifying examination; this exam provides a uniform national standard in that AICPA develops it for many state boards.

ABA's and AMA's basic codes are primarily ethical rather than technical, but state and local legal and medical societies provide important assistance in considering standards of practice and in structuring peer review committees to address questions of competence as well as ethics.

The American Optometric Association, St. Louis, conducts a program that accredits professional degree programs at schools of optometry and residency and paraoptometric programs. Its Council on Optometric Education, recognized by the U.S. Department of Education as *the* operating body for accreditation, works to "safeguard the public from educational programs of unacceptable quality."[11]

The American Dental Association (ADA) accredits programs in dentistry "to ensure quality education for members of the professions and thus protection of the public which they serve." Dental schools voluntarily participate in the program, but most state dental boards require graduation from an accredited program and all dental schools seek this accreditation. ADA manages several programs to ensure a high standard of care; these range from peer review boards, to analyses of the effect of insurance programs on care, to observation of practices in private dental offices. In fact, when ADA was founded in 1859, one of the founders' chief concerns was "the establishment of qualifying criteria and standards for dental practitioners," and one of its first activities "was a campaign to establish state dental examining and licensing boards."[12]

Less Technical Occupations

Associations also play a significant role in forming standards and certifying competence in some of the less technical occupations. In addition to its detailed code of ethics, the Public Relations Society of America has a voluntary accreditation program, in part to preempt government licensing action. The program requires the candidate to have at least five years of experience and to pass oral and written examinations in order to "attest to a professional's competency in the practice of public relations."[13]

The Society of Real Estate Appraisers, Chicago, and the Institute of Chartered Financial Analysts, Charlottesville, Virginia, manage certification programs, as does the American Society of Chartered Life Underwriters, Bryn Mawr, Pennsylvania. Indeed, insurance associations and the nonprofit Insurance Training Institute have detailed and complex programs to create and ensure professional courses that lead to certificates and associate diplomas in various specialities and to the professional designation of Chartered Property Casualty Underwriter. This designation requires candidates to pass a series of lengthy written examinations.

Awarded certificates are generally intended to indicate that the holder meets established professional standards judged by peer review. The American Society of Interior Designers, New York, requires prospective members to pass a two-day examination covering blueprints, color theory, design theory, architectural materials, and the like.

A Mixed Blessing?

It is not universally agreed that association involvement in creating and encouraging professional standards is an unmixed blessing. Doubts can become strong when standards move from the voluntary realm of certification to accreditation and, especially, to mandatory licensing requirements. Some argue that mandated levels of education keep some people from practicing an occupation. Costs are driven up, it is argued, false occupational distinctions are created, and the compensating benefits are small, if they exist at all. The whole structure of professionalism, in this view, results primarily in increased income for professionals by artificially limiting the number of practitioners. The increased competence and safety that constitute the rationale are not the genuine or, at least, not the only reasons professionals wish to be licensed; even if these are the only reasons, competence can be promoted without restrictive licensing.

From this perspective, much of the work of a bar association is to prevent the unauthorized practice of law, not merely for the sake of public safety but to keep for lawyers business that others could do. Much of the AMA's work is intended to restrict other practitioners, such as osteopaths or nurses, who could perform all or many medical functions. The harm, indeed, is done largely to those who cannot afford full professional services.

Associations sometimes do oppose licensing. DSA "opposes occupational licensing concepts" because licensing chills competition, is ultimately inflationary, unduly subverts the free market, and does not eliminate consumer abuses.[14]

The preceding arguments concentrate especially on the full legal control that some licensing affords, although they generally recognize the utility of giving consumers signals of professional competence to offset their lack of knowledge. Arguments that emphasize the limit that licensing places on market activity often stem from the same economic perspective that acknowledges the importance of information in complex markets. The result is that objections are made against government licensing, but not against certification and registration. In fact, foes of licensing argue that milder programs retain the benefits of encouraging competence without restricting the rights to practice.[15]

Association programs that encourage genuine standards of competent performance and certify competent practitioners are more generous than government certification in allowing consumers the option of choosing certified ability. The consumer does not have to select a certified interior designer or a certified association executive and may instead decide to purchase the services of the uncertified. But, if they wish, consumers can choose to take seriously the implied claim of greater competence and study.

In many ways the situation regarding consumers' choices is similar for association-accredited degree and education programs. The most one might say in criticism is that certification and accreditation create a web of complexity, making success more difficult than it should be for uncertified workers. Consumers, however, still retain the option of doubting the claims implied in certification.

When broadly considering the traditional professions that began to be licensed in the United States in the mid-19th century, it is clear that growing technical complexity makes the public's advance knowledge of the adequacy of services ever more difficult to obtain without a strong signal of educational attainment and professional competence. The public, through its elected officials, has therefore shown little inclination to eliminate the safety that licensing affords. At the same time, however, some functions historically performed by advanced professionals are increasingly being taken over by others. Dispute resolution services and financial planning that do not involve lawyers or CPAs are two examples. Taken together, these two trends indicate ongoing needs in some areas for licensing or other strict measures and decreased needs in others.

ENDNOTES

1. *Washington Post*, October 15, 1989, Outlook section.

2. San Francisco Medical Society, *New Member Handbook* (San Francisco: San Francisco Medical Society, no date), 24-26.

3. American Medical Association, "Principles of Medical Ethics," in ibid.

4. Public Relations Society of America, *Code of Professional Standards for the Practice of Public Relations* (Washington, D.C.: PRSA, no date).

5. National Association of Mutual Insurance Agents, "Code of Ethics," in *Ethics Background Kit* (Washington, D.C.: American Society of Association Executives, no date), 75.

6. Public Relations Society of America, *Code*.

7. Lewis Galambos, *Competition and Cooperation* (Baltimore: The Johns Hopkins Press, 1966), 283.

8. Neil H. Offen, "The Direct Selling Association's Consumer Protection Code of Ethics," in *Proceedings of the White House Conference on Self Regulation* (Washington, D.C.: American Society of Association Executives, 1984), 33-44 *passim*.

9. Ibid.

10. Council of Engineering and Scientific Society Executives, *Science Engineering and Altruism—Non-profit Societies Serving America* (Draft) (Washington, D.C.: CESSE June 1989).

11. "Award to the American Optometric Association," in *Proceedings*, 83.

12. John L. Bomba, "Remarks of Dr. John L. Bomba," in *Proceedings*, 46.

13. Public Relations Society of America, untitled pamphlet (Washington, D.C.: PRSA, no date).

14. Offen, *Proceedings*.

15. S. David Young, *The Rule of Experts* (Washington, D.C.: Cato Institute, 1987).

 # Research and Statistics

KEY FINDINGS

- ☐ Almost two-thirds of associations collect statistics or engage in research.
- ☐ Statistical efforts benefit the public by giving government basic facts and by providing comparative data that enable producers to improve.
- ☐ The research efforts of associations, especially those of learned societies, define the scope and standards of entire fields.

"Association statistics are the basis for much of the government's information."

The statistics that associations gather enable similar businesses to compare their output, productivity, and costs. Association research programs range from managing the professional peer review of articles, to reporting basic research, through product and ingredient testing. Both research and statistics help association members to better manage their own activities by providing benchmarks of comparison and excellence and by generating new information.

Nearly 65 percent of the associations surveyed gather statistics and facilitate or engage in research, comprising nearly 75 percent each of trade associations and cause-related and advocacy groups and 54 percent of professional associations. As with public information, total sums spent are large, amounting to more than $2 billion in direct expenditures and $67 million worth of volunteer effort. The distinction between research and, say, education or public information contained in journals is not always clearly delineated, but the large order of magnitude of the effort is clear.

The research and statistical activities of associations benefit the general public in much the same way they benefit members. First, statistics that associations gather about member activities form the basis for much of the government's information. Central facts about profits and expenditures within an industry govern intelligent public and investment policy affecting that industry. Second, statistics enabling one producer to compare his or her activities with others allow that producer to improve performance by setting expectations and goals. If the industry's products are in the open market, then producing them more efficiently is a common benefit.

Third, the research programs of professional associations are central to the very mission and definition of the professions. Most national associations of academics, for example, publish professional journals renowned as the most prestigious in their field. Because they serve as a forum for publishing research findings, these journals provide incentive to conduct research. More importantly, they incorporate a process of peer review that sets important research directions, helps to validate findings, and generally defines the scope, standards, and current tendencies within a field.

This function serves a society beyond the professional members if understanding the underlying subject matter is at all useful to the general public. The utility is most evident in the natural and biological sciences and economics. Technical mastery of nature and economic mastery of the business cycle have brought about much of the comfort, wealth, and extended life span that characterizes the modern material condition. This mastery is a function of thought and research, technologically and politically implemented. Structures advancing this research are, therefore, of central importance in undergirding our daily lives; the process of peer review is central among these structures.

Research in the social sciences and humanities is also significant. Forming the basis of much scholarship at the heart of graduate and undergraduate training, such research at its best allows a fuller experience of the art, music, literature, and thought that elevates the spirit. Research in psychology and social sciences other than economics forms the foundation supporting business and management education and thus improves the organizational, marketing, and motivational techniques that drive modern management. Professional associations are key structures that focus and direct this research, as they manage the peer review process and publications that orient and help to define professional activities.

Trade associations and cause-related and advocacy groups also facilitate and direct research. In these instances, research directly funded or conducted by association members and staff serves a common association interest and, therefore, the economic or social sector with which the association is concerned. An outstanding example is research into the toxic properties of chemicals, to be discussed later in this section.

STATISTICS

Many associations gather basic statistics in the form of operating ratio reports. A good example is the American Society of Association Executives (ASAE), Washington, D.C. ASAE's *Association Operating Ratio Report* allows executives to compare their associations' income and expenses to others.[1] Survey responses of ASAE members are grouped according to their associations' geographical type, structure (individual or corporate), and economic and professional sector. Income and expenses are categorized by function and in standard accounting object classes. Using the statistics as a basis of comparison, executives can adjust their planning and spending accordingly in order to manage their finances more prudently and function more efficiently.

Some statistical information is made available in other comparative forms. The Society of Independent Gasoline Marketers of America (SIGMA), Washington, D.C., for example, compiles a yearly, "in-depth survey of SIGMA members' operations, sales, and services."[2] The report furnishes a member profile, indicating the typical amount of fuel supplied, the typical number of outlets owned and people employed, the amount of new construction and remodeling, the sources of fuel for independent marketers, and the numbers and types of stations operated and supplied. The report also analyzes average fuel sales, percentages of fuel types sold, amounts of fuel blended with ethanol, and amounts of nonfuel sales, such as tobacco and soft drinks. This information is the single most comprehensive set of facts about a significant segment of the fuel business.

Representing more than 500,000 small businesses, the National Federation of Independent Business (NFIB), Washington, D.C., does extensive survey work issued in the form of quarterly and monthly statistical reports about capital expenditures, inventories sales, and other business conditions. These statistics are not kept as a separate category by the federal government. NFIB also samples its members about the future: What changes do they expect in employment levels, prices, and capital expenditures? What do small businessowners think about general economic conditions?

The National Association of Purchasing Management (NAPM), Oradell, New Jersey, does a monthly business report based on survey data and explanations about planned changes in production, inventories, new orders, employment, prices, and capital expenditures. The timeliness and confidentiality of the report, widely regarded by government and the media as a highly credible economic forecast, would be difficult to match through another mechanism.

The Better Home Heat Council provides a utility reporting service that "monitors national gas rates and fuel adjustment charges for each gas utility in Massachusetts," giving members current facts about the comparative costs of heating homes with gas. This information is useful in marketing efforts.[3]

The American Institute of Physics, New York, provides statistics on scientific manpower to the U.S. Departments of Energy and Defense, the National Aeronautics and Space Administration, the National Science Foundation, state and local governments, and private entities. The information covers an array of manpower issues, including the supply of and demand for women and minorities in physics careers. In addition, the data are used to reform curricula in high schools, colleges, and universities.

RESEARCH

These examples of association statistical contributions are matched by the many instances in which associations facilitate and direct research. Most of the major academic associations, for example, publish scholarly journals, which are their most important ongoing activity. While these journals serve as resources in which to report research and elaborate and dissect arguments, more significantly, for many researchers they are the most prestigious publications in which to appear. The *American Political Science Review* and the *Proceedings of the Modern Language Association* are *the* places in which a political scientist or scholar of English literature seeks to publish.

Because of their prestige, the journals, through their editors, are responsible for upholding and even setting standards of accuracy and excellence within an entire discipline, for adjusting and supporting the relative importance of subfields within disciplines, and for encouraging or discouraging novel approaches and lines of inquiry. Indeed, they also serve to bind the discipline together as a unit, along with other basic association activities such as conventions. Debates about a discipline's structure are carried out through discussions and decisions about the apportionment of articles. Scholarly disciplines, then, especially to the degree they engage in basic research, are largely defined by national associations through their leading scholarly journals.

The research journals of learned associations go beyond the journals of most other associations because of their central role in creating and sustaining the scholarly ethos of the entire activity. They do more than convey information or publish research results: They are part of the structure of reward and approval that sustains basic research.

The role of scholarly and other associations in facilitating research is complemented by many direct research activities either performed by staff or, more

"Association research is often extraordinarily useful."

frequently, by supervising grants and contracts. As mentioned previously, the Cosmetic, Toiletry and Fragrance Association (CFTA) evaluates the safety of ingredients in a program to develop new testing methods and other scientific techniques. The independent, scientific Cosmetic Ingredient Review (CIR) group judges available data, with CFTA coordinating necessary additional research. A typical summary of a CIR conclusion gives a fuller sense of their activities.

> The Panel reviewed information supplied on AMP/AMPD, including additional data made available by the supplier of the ingredient in response to requests from the Team. Because data on irritation and sensitization was limited to results from testing on products containing the ingredient at less than 1%, the Panel noted that it would limit the conclusion to indicate that the use of this ingredient in products was safe at 1% concentration. . . . If there are any companies interested in using the ingredient at concentrations higher than 1%, they should submit irritation and sensitization data demonstrating the safety of the ingredient at higher concentrations.[4]

Another trade association engaged in extensive research is the Chemical Manufacturers Association (CMA). As with the CFTA, much of CMA's research and related advocacy are devoted to handling or mitigating government regulations, especially those of the U.S. Environmental Protection Agency (EPA). CMA spent more than $7.5 million in FY 1988 on the effort, nearly 60 percent of which was earmarked for research.

Much of CMA's research focuses on the health effects of chemicals, determined by various contracted toxicological, epidemiological, and clinical studies. Other research examines environmental and atmospheric issues and includes risk analyses. The panel on fluorocarbons, for example, spent more than $1 million on its overall activities designed to investigate and comment on the issue of fluorocarbons in the atmosphere. Of this, $380,000 was committed to an international effort to study stratospheric ozone.

Sometimes associations unite their research efforts. The American Petroleum Institute, Washington, D.C., for example, participated with CMA in an animal toxicology research program to examine various effects of benzene. The storage and disposal of polychlorinated biphenys (PCBs), an issue of great interest to EPA, was studied by CMA in conjunction with several organizations, including the National Electrical Manufacturers Association, the Association of American Railroads, and the Environmental Defense Fund, all of Washington, D.C. Research may also be conducted to set standards. CMA's panel on water additives worked with EPA and the National Sanitation Foundation, Ann Arbor, Michigan, to begin a program to set water additive standards.

Such research efforts draw upon the knowledge of scientists from member companies, with scientific panels chaired by an appropriate expert. One may wonder what leads associations, rather than individual companies, to undertake research. In general, CMA's research considers the public or external effects of chemicals and, therefore, goes beyond the immediate market concerns of any individual company. In the same way, research panels constitute a forum for industry-wide response to actual and proposed public regulation. CMA's research efforts belong to the same broad category in which associations act on collective production issues that are insufficiently handled through individual market decisions. Research is a mechanism through which the association mediates public concerns to the industry when the normal response through market performance and individual political effort would be inadequate. Research is also an obvious mechanism to affect the legislative and regulatory formulation regarding these concerns.[5]

In response to the discovery in 1987 that nitrosamine compounds are formed through unwanted reactions when cosmetics are manufactured or stored, CFTA began to study these potentially powerful carcinogens. The work of CFTA's task force led to publication of a major research report and funding of a major research program through the Midwest Research Institute. These, along with other, efforts led the cosmetic industry to identify ways to inhibit nitrosamine formation in model formulation systems. The research addressed an industry-wide problem within a structure of public and government concern.

The goals of the research and statistical programs conducted by the Association of American Railroads (AAR), Washington, D.C., are to reduce injuries, meet regulatory requirements, and enhance the efficiency of railroad operations. To these ends, AAR prepares financial reports for the public and the U.S. Interstate Commerce Commission, comprising commodity and transport statistics, ten-year industry trends, and the cost of capital in the industry; examines the materials and components in locomotives and freight and passenger cars; studies the productivity of freight car fleets; and researches various energy and environmental questions. The association also manages large research facilities in Colorado and Illinois and tracks the location of every freight car in the country, so cars can be sent where needed.

Professional and other associations with individual, rather than corporate, members also engage in direct research. The Public Relations Society of America initiates research, develops techniques and reports, and answers more than 20,000 requests a year at its Research Information Center. The American Physical Therapy Association promotes basic and clinical research in physical therapy by enhancing graduate education programs, offering special research awards, and evaluating research papers for presentation at the annual conference. In addition, it conducts surveys and organizes data in order to keep accurate statistics and trends about the physical therapy profession.

"Many advocacy and cause-related organizations are involved in research."

The Healthcare Forum is an example of an association that shares elements of both trade and professional groups. Here, research directly benefits members and, through them, the public. In 1988, the Forum co-sponsored a project to investigate ways to reduce the turnover of registered nurses in hospitals. Turnover of nurses is a major problem: R.N. vacancies have doubled since 1983, and hospitals spend on average $20,000 to replace a registered nurse. More than this, the shortage of nurses adversely affects the quality of patient care. The study investigated 15 hospitals of varying sizes and, through interviews and mathematical prioritizing, identified key impediments to successful retention and recruiting in each hospital. The hospitals then formed task groups to devise personnel, organizational, and resource strategies to deal with the central obstacles.

Many advocacy and cause-related organizations are involved in research. The National Council of Jewish Women, New York, began in 1963 a pilot program that later became the federal Retired Senior Volunteer Program. In 1965, the Council established a Research Institute to study education at the Hebrew University; in 1974 and 1975, it surveyed day-care facilities and the juvenile justice system; in 1985, it conducted studies of working parents; and in 1987, it evaluated child abuse programs. Several of the initiatives were launched with outside funding.

The American Association of University Women (AAUW) initiated in 1989 a combined program to support teaching sabbaticals and to eliminate "barriers to girls' and women's participation in education," to promote "the value of diversity and cross-cultural communication," and to promote "greater understanding of how women and girls think, learn, work, and play."

The research agenda AAUW is now promoting through its 1,900 branches intends to consider discrimination in curricula, intervention for what the association calls "girls at risk," and ethnic groups' ignorance of one another.

These activities frame the scope and purpose of association-based research. The research topics are as varied as the social viewpoints associations express and the work in which they engage. Much of the research either addresses the economic concerns of the members or aims to advance the cause or group. These motives, however, do not detract from the social value of association research, for the research typically involves a public matter, and its value stems from the accuracy and validity that research adds to public discussion of important issues.

The research facilitated by learned societies normally extends beyond specific public issues. It is broader and more basic. Such research buttresses the interests of association members, whose profession is largely defined by and whose careers are vitally connected to research. In these instances, occasional questions arise about relevance; still, the basic research facilitated by many associations is often extraordinarily useful and, arguably, desirable in and of itself.

ENDNOTES

1. American Society of Association Executives, *Association Operating Ratio Report*, 8th ed. (Washington, D.C.: ASAE, 1989).
2. Society of Independent Gasoline Marketers Association, *Statistical Report* (Washington, D.C.: SIGMA, 1988).
3. Better Home Heat Council, *What It is, What It Does for Me and Why I Support It* (Wellesley Hills, MA: Better Home Heat Council, no date).
4. Cosmetic, Toiletry and Fragrance Association, *CIR Developments*, January 12, 1989.
5. Chemical Manufacturers Association, *Special Programs, 1987-88*, (Washington, D.C.: CMA, 1988).

 # Political Education and Government Relations

KEY FINDINGS

- Associations are actively involved in political education and government relations, but the percentage that earmark funds for this activity—32 percent—is surprisingly low.
- The political education and government relations programs of associations serve a public purpose by disseminating information to legislatures and administrative agencies, by checking the private interests of other groups, and by providing an opportunity for citizens to exercise political responsibility and control.
- Much of the public value afforded by political involvement depends upon associations responsibly pursuing their collective interests—that is, their responsibly keeping in mind the overall health of political conditions that nurture liberal democratic government at the same time as they press their own causes.

"The amount associations spend on political education is smaller than many might believe."

Associations lobby legislators, meet with government officials, and hire attorneys. They fund campaigns, pay honoraria to listen to congressmen, and help their industries, professions, and causes wade through a maze of regulations. More national associations are headquartered in Washington, D.C., than in any other city, and many state associations are located in state capitals. They are there because they need to talk to government, not because the air is especially clean or the cost of living especially low.

The political activity of associations hardly wins universal praise. When one reads about special interests, trade associations come to mind; when one hears of lobbyists gathering in committee chambers as bills are written and deals are cut, association lobbyists are there. Yet, associations are not always on the same side of every issue. Indeed some, association competes with others on virtually every issue. Newspaper publishers and telephone companies disagree about electronic information. Music publishers and electronics manufacturers differ about digital taping systems. Independent gasoline distributors hardly share every interest with major chains. Within industries and among providers of broadly related products, there are sharp disagreements. Producers of competing products have individual interests that diverge significantly.

Many cause-related and advocacy associations lobby for social legislation that affects their group or concerns them politically. These associations lobby at roughly the same rate as trade and professional groups, and their actions are often meant to effect massive social change. They, too, clash with each other. While one may oppose specific positions, these associations' right to participate politically would not be denied. Indeed, when people consider the full range of associations, they see how often they believe that associations' political activity often has public utility; this utility, however, is inseparable from the same moderation of self-interest and consideration of healthy public conditions that govern responsible individual behavior.

More than 32 percent of the associations surveyed spend funds on political education, comprising 43 percent of trade associations, 25 percent of professional associations, and 26 percent of cause-related and advocacy groups. Thirty-nine percent of trade associations use volunteers in this activity, compared with 21 percent of professional and 15 percent of cause-related and advocacy groups.

The total amount spent on and the proportion of associations involved in political education are smaller than many might believe. Trade associations spend roughly 6 percent of total expenditures on political education, professional associations less than 2 percent, and cause-related and advocacy groups roughly 3 percent. Some portion of the funds spent on administration and fund-raising goes to political education, but even so, the numbers are surprisingly low. Even among trade associations, a greater proportion are engaged in education (86 percent), research (73 percent), public information (73 percent), and setting performance and safety standards (50 percent) than in political education.

Political education and government relations serve a collective private interest. Associations gather together and provide cohesion for those whom others, like government, treat identically under law and regulation. In facing government, associations' first task is to represent the collective interests of their members in order to win favorable sales, tax treatment, laws, or regulations.

Yet, as natural as this seems, it is not altogether acceptable. One expects or, at least, urges individuals to vote for and encourage legislators devoted to enhancing the common good through fair taxes, just laws, sensible regulations, and intelligent budget decisions, whether or not these serve the individual's immediate interests. Why should associations, whose right to act politically is essential in a liberal democracy, be exempt from the same injunctions? The nation's founders did not construct a regime whose success depends on angelic devotion to common interests. Somehow, the common good is to be largely consonant with and supported by selfish interests. The hope is that those pursuing individual and collective interests will, as they clash, responsibly understand when those interests must be moderated to accomplish public goals and support generally desirable political conditions. A strategic perspective for the long run must accompany short-term interests.

COUNTERING OTHER VIEWS

This suggests that the political activities of associations can serve a public interest or have public value in several ways. First, associations' participation in the political process is necessary to counter other associations. Public policy is always to some degree the result of insistent private representation and requests. It never simply results from the public interest conceived in isolation from its effects on particular people, places, and economic sectors. In order for public policy to consider these interests broadly and to ensure that no one of them dominates, the interplay of associations is necessary.

As they pursue a collective private interest, associations thus serve a public interest by checking other collective private interests. What is necessary beyond this balancing is attention to the general context of political representation, lest intense, competitive, private lobbying overcomes all explicit consideration of the common good. This context embodies fairness, honesty, and a sense of broad concerns that moderate the simple dominance of one's own narrow interest.

"If associations did not represent their interests, other interests would triumph."

One expects industries to lobby for import quotas and chemical companies to lobby for a minimum of regulation. But one also wants from them some sense of the general conditions of economic competitiveness and of the general need to deal with external effects, such as environmental pollution, since they, too, seek life enhanced by economic growth, social well-being, and physical health. A short-range perspective focusing only on immediate problems is foolish. If associations represent their interests in a narrow and extreme manner, they invite the same from their foes, and the general climate becomes one of extreme distrust, where compromise is difficult.

Yet, if associations did not represent their interests at all, other interests would triumph and produce results that the public would not choose. Political action by associations can usefully moderate other interests and in a way that provides additional public utility if it respects general conditions of economic growth, democratic political choice, and social and physical health. Indeed, because associations often effect compromises of the views of individual members and strive to establish overall conditions needed by their industry, profession, or cause, they may employ broader perspectives than any individual member.

DISSEMINATING INFORMATION

A second way in which associations' political activity may serve a broad public interest is by providing information to congressmen and officials of the executive branch. Sensible government must understand the effects of its actions—present or future. It cannot rest contentedly with dreams or hopes of intended outcomes and results. Given the complexity of professions and industries, and with all parts of the economy increasingly intertwined, it is difficult for government to know all possible results of intended actions. How will a particular tax policy affect incentives? How will a change in Medicare affect behavior? Can industry adapt practices to respond to health, safety, the environment, and discrimination at little cost, or will the cost be substantial? Some grasp of costs and benefits is required for prudent legislation or regulation, but it is difficult to achieve this grasp without listening to those who will be affected. Therefore, legislatures and regulatory bodies typically hold hearings, where associations and others may supply information about the real effects of proposals.

Because any lobbyist or citizen can use special knowledge to misinform by holding back or exaggerating, no legislator should depend on only one group for information. But this caveat does not erase the need to talk to experts to trace the potential effects of a bill. One way to do this that maximizes one's chances for receiving a broad picture of affected interests is to talk to the relevant associations.

TENDING TO THE GRASSROOTS

A third function of political activity is that of providing a training ground for wider local or national political involvement. As they seek to meet their collective interests, associations can give their members a sophisticated understanding of actual political process, helping to develop the special abilities needed to participate. Local neighborhood and educational groups, for example, often spawn people who seek higher office, and ongoing political involvement through their associations can help members construct political views about how affairs should or should not change. The compromise and judgment necessary to effect a common position among associates mirror the abilities needed to effect the common good at the state or national level.

Through the political process, associations forcefully remind government representatives of their constituents' interests. Associations are a central mechanism through which constituents mobilize and are heard on issues. Without the organized expression of constituent demands, representatives tend to substitute their own opinions or the opinions of those who are most insistent. Popular government means that the people must be heard, even if their wishes are not followed. Associations are among the institutions that mediate between separate individuals and potentially despotic government and that lead individuals to compromise their immediate wishes to formulate thoughtful collective interests.

A negative side emerges when constituents become mere pressure groups, forcing upon representatives narrow notions that are not subject to compromise. The difference between formulating and expressing genuine collective interest and pressuring for narrow results with no attention to the common good is neither hard and fast nor simple to state, but it is real. A cacophony of narrow interests that does not responsibly consider long-range conditions and necessities makes intelligent compromise and decision difficult. However, without hearing constituents' interests, forcefully expressed, government can too easily ignore all but a few voices.

Associations' political activity, then, can be valuable by countering other potentially narrow interests, by bringing information before representatives, by training members in democratic processes and political give-and-take, and by formulating and expressing constituents' demands. Specific examples help to illustrate these points.

EXAMPLES OF POLITICAL ACTIVITY

The American Hotel and Motel Association includes government relations as the fourth element of its basic mission "to foster conditions in which the lodging industry will be free to operate profitably; to promote tourism and high-quality hospitality services; to provide rewarding opportunities for people working in the lodging industry; to represent, through an active government affairs program, the views and concerns of the membership."[1] Through the government affairs program, the association solicits funds for a political action committee and political education fund, tracks and discusses congressional issues, coordinates member efforts to improve grass-roots lobbying of congressmen through constituent hotels and

"Through the political process, associations remind government representatives of constitutents' interests."

members, and works with state associations to improve their lobbying efforts. One action now being explored is the expansion of information services, testimony, and studies that can support state legislative affairs.

Another example is the Kentucky Municipal League, Lexington, an association of 300 Kentucky cities. The association develops a legislative package for each state legislative session and tends to it carefully. The general goal is to redirect some of the energies and funds from state to local government. "During the 1988 legislative session," the president reports, "we enjoyed a number of successes, but perhaps most importantly, continued to maintain the integrity of our legislative program by providing honest and forthright information to members of the Kentucky General Assembly and to the press about the issues and concerns that we face in our cities."[2] League leaders meet with Kentucky legislative leaders and call on their members to meet with members of the Kentucky General Assembly and engage in "hard-nosed politics in order to get the job done."[3]

The League's political activities often produce innovative results. In 1987, for example, a municipal-pool bond issue was developed that provides a substantial revenue source for cities.

The League's political activities are remindful of the realities of political and association life. The League represents cities, that is, it already has a public interest in view when it acts. But this public view is not identical with the full public interest. For example, the League is investigating joint legislative activities with the Kentucky Association of Counties, Frankfort, as part of its efforts to interest state government in local issues. This example is only to emphasize that the interest of states are not identical with those of cities, and neither interest is identical with the national interest. A rich interplay of viewpoints and political efforts is the material of political decision. It calls for intelligent compromise, but without effective representation, some interests will not be sufficiently considered, including parts of the public interest.

Professional associations, as well as trade groups, often conduct a full range of political activities. The American Physical Therapy Association, Alexandria, Virginia, for example, "represents the interest of physical therapists at the state and federal levels." It attempts to effect changes in Medicare regulations and resolve reimbursement issues by working with the U.S. Department of Health and Human Services. It influences federal legislation to aid education programs for physical therapy students. It deals with state insurance commissions and compensation boards, attempting to secure legislation mandating easy physical access to buildings and related benefits for the clientele of physical therapists.

As with licensing activities, one may argue that the public interest is better served by containing medical costs and restricting government spending on education. But how best to apportion the overall health and disability budget among different areas of health care is neither simply obvious, nor plain. The public value of political representation comes from healthy debate, accurate information, and balancing of interests and constituent pressures that allow legislators to make sophisticated judgments about the common interest.

The Florida chapter of the National Association of Social Workers, Tallahassee, acts on legislation and manages a political action group. Legislative action is effected through a lobbyist and involves testifying before legislative committees and at regulatory hearings. The goal is to "promote the passage and implementation of positive human services legislation, rules and regulations." The "political action for candidate election" group has a similar goal of advancing "the cause of quality human services in Florida."[4]

These actions embody the interests both of professionals and clients. One result was enactment in 1982 of a statute that licensed mental health professionals and in 1987 of a statute that created a state Board of Clinical Social Work, Marriage and Family Therapy and Mental Health Counseling to administer the application and licensure process. A Certified Master Social Worker category was also created, administered by Florida's Department of Professional Regulation.

Legislative activity of this sort embraces goals similar to those found in trade associations. The actions strive to create positive legislation, in the form of "the best possible legal regulation for social workers."

Does this type of legislative activity have public value? As noted previously, some economists question the desirability of many licensing arrangements, but it is very difficult to separate the public health value of professional licensing and state certification from the private economic interests they serve. One practical way of drawing the line is through open, competitive politics, legislative hearings, and regulatory decisions. The political activity of professional associations that seek favorable regulation can bring to bear information, concerns, and sophistication that otherwise might be missed. As long as these considerations are honestly expressed and allow opportunity for contrasting assessments, the public interest can be served by enabling laws to be enacted on the basis of genuine understanding. Many legislative bodies might downplay social welfare issues unless made continually aware of them.

The Cosmetic, Toiletry and Fragrance Association (CFTA) publishes a legislative bulletin describing the association's involvement in significant state and federal legislative developments. In 1988, these activities ranged from testifying at congressional subcommittee hearings and countering restrictive animal testing legislation (which was defeated or contained in five states), to dealing with laws or proposed laws on household products, clean air, and cosmetology. Before the House Small Business Subcommittee on Regulation and Business Opportunity, CFTA's president argued that the safety record of cosmetics, the effectiveness of voluntary programs, and the wide range of existing Food and Drug Administration controls negated charges that cosmetic safety is inadequate.

In Illinois, Maryland, Massachusetts, New Jersey, and Pennsylvania, CFTA and its members opposed legislation to restrict animal testing. These efforts were instrumental in defeating the proposals. CFTA also worked to help shape congressional revision of the trademark law so that several objectionable provisions were dropped.[5]

The scope of this activity helps clarify why effective association political activity, based on clearly presented information, serves a useful public purpose. If Congress is to regulate, say, animal testing, it must be informed about the effect of proposals on other desirable activities, such as testing the safety of products.

The Chemical Manufacturers Association (CMA) has mounted a program to strengthen the political programs of member companies and to build grassroots advocacy on legislative and regulatory issues. Various association committees and task forces organize nearly 2,000 yearly meetings to devise a combined technical, media, and government relations strategy on relevant issues. The stated purpose of the program is "to constructively address ill-conceived government proposals and anticipate actions that industry should take before such proposals are made." This "has resulted in member companies helping public officials develop legislation and regulations that benefit society and the chemical industry. Examples are apparent in the debate on Superfund and tax reform...."[6]

In the case of Superfund, the current law "spreads hazardous waste cleanup obligations among other industries

"Political education can include disseminating general information."

more equitably than the original Superfund law did." This "is a direct result of CMA's involvement in the legislative and regulatory process."[7]

In the case of the 1986 tax bill, CMA worked successfully with others to offset repeal of the investment tax credit by extending tax credits for research and development and achieving "favorable accelerated depreciation rates."[8]

To the degree that these pieces of legislation were improved or that one believes industries must be able to influence how they are regulated and controlled, these efforts serve a public interest. Attempts to influence the political process are best controlled through political competition and self-restraint, not through restricting what is useful in association political activity.

As mentioned, political education sometimes takes the form of disseminating general information. The Water Pollution Control Federation, for example, conducts tours of water treatment plants for congressmen and their staffs. The Renewable Natural Resources Foundation, Bethesda, Maryland, conducts forums for and offers journal subscriptions to appropriate congressional staff, attempting to provide scientific, nonpartisan analysis. The American Society for Microbiology, Washington, D.C., recommends policy actions to Congress and regulatory agencies.

Cause-related and advocacy associations also are deeply immersed in political activities. The National Council of Jewish Women produces an "advocacy action package," comprising a quarterly *Washington Newsletter*, a legislative update published eight to 10 times a year when Congress is in session, and "coalition building guidelines."

Legislative efforts of the American Association of University Women (AAUW), include devoting an issue of its quarterly *Leader in Action* to "lobbying for a change." This attempt to educate members in lobbying techniques contains the "Ten Commandments of Lobbying," listed next.

Successful lobbyists, whether paid professionals or citizen activists, always keep the following in mind:

    I Know your facts; express them.
    II Know your opposition.
    III Correct errors immediately.
    IV Plan, coordinate, and follow up.
    V Avoid being a zealot.
    VI Cultivate your allies.

VII Know the legislative process.
VIII Be careful with money.
  IX Grow thick skin.
  X Win.[9]

These rules are then described in greater detail, using specific examples and backed up with general resource manuals and specific materials. The materials include position papers on "child care, economic equity, family planning, pay equity, reproductive choice, the Title X family planning program and United Nations reform." Meant to aid members in securing changes supporting a liberal agenda, the materials reveal a sophisticated understanding of the potential of legislative efforts:

> Legislative successes can be measured by many things other than the passage and signing of a bill, from finally getting your point across to a legislator who seemed intransigent to adding another 10 cosponsors to a bill during a particular legislative session, to holding a hearing in a crucial aspect of a bill. AAUW's legislative victories during recent years [together with other groups] include, for example, not only passage of the Civil Rights Restoration Act and defeat of Judge Robert Bork's nomination to the U.S. Supreme Court but the fact that bills in child care, family leave and pay equity are now going concerns after a decade of lobbying, with real possibilities of passage during the 101st Congress. And even if no progress is made on your priority bill, success can be measured by new strategies discovered.[10]

One might disagree with these positions or with the notion that they generally represent the views of university women, but reasonably and fairly representing views and developing people's political skill and abilities are legitimate public functions.

Association political activity, then, is a reasonable part of the nation's political life, providing balance and information, mobilizing constituencies, and honing political skills. It can be subject to abuse, in part because of the way in which political institutions function, but that is a complex topic in its own right and beyond the scope of this report.

ENDNOTES

1. American Hotel and Motel Association, *Strategic Plan*, 1989, 1990 (Washington, D.C.: AHMA).

2. Kentucky Municipal League, *Annual Report, 1989* (Lexington: Kentucky Municipal League, 1989).

3. In addition to its annual report, the Kentucky Municipal League publishes a monthly, *The Kentucky City.*

4. See the brochure of the National Association of Social Workers, Inc., Florida Chapter; and also *Florida PACE,* no date.

5. Cosmetic, Toiletry and Fragrance Association, *Legislative Bulletin,* December 2, 1988.

6. Chemical Manufacturers Association, *What It Is, What It Does* (Washington, D.C.: CMA, no date).

7. Ibid.

8. Ibid.

9. American Association of University Women, *Leader in Action* 9 (Spring 1989).

10. Ibid.

★ ★ ★ ★ Community Service

KEY FINDINGS

□ Nearly 20 percent of associations are involved in providing community service, which constitutes the largest use of volunteer time among all association efforts.

□ Associations can be especially useful vehicles for providing community service because they mobilize and focus the talents of many individuals and firms.

□ The public value of associations' service contributions are best secured when they stem from a connection to the skills and interests that associations represent.

"Associations are well suited to mobilize members for community service."

Community service constituted the largest use of volunteer time among all association efforts—nearly 100 million hours—and drew volunteers from one-quarter of the associations surveyed. Within the survey universe, 19 percent of the associations participated in community service projects, including 10 percent of trade associations, 23 percent of professional associations, and 36 percent of cause-related and advocacy associations. Several associations even define their missions as primarily that of community service.

The purposes behind associations' community service are twofold: (1) to achieve a useful result, for example, helping those in need or advancing public education and (2) to receive recognition for these good works.

Associations usually engage in community service tied reasonably closely to their members' trade or profession, but they also sometimes devote themselves to a need beyond their immediate expertise.

The social value of community service is sufficiently clear and noncontroversial that it does not require extensive analysis here. Only two issues arise. The first concerns the relationship between community service and government activity: Is community service merely a useful adjunct to that which government should provide, or does it play a more fundamental role in motivating and organizing citizens to help others and themselves? Without taking a stand on this issue, it is fair to point out that associations have been deeply involved in the upsurge in service called for in the Reagan and Bush administrations, which see this service as basic, not merely desirable.

The second issue concerns whether community service can be conducted in a way that validates and supports the association's basic mission without implicitly agreeing that this mission is undesirable. Expressed another way, is community service evidence of a guilty conscience, or it is a generous expression of the skills, abilities, and activities that associations and their members support? This latter affirmative outlook foots useful community service on the steadier base. The examples of community service which follow are those supporting associations' basic missions or flowing from their interests and understanding.

FILLING SPECIFIC NEEDS

Associations are especially well suited to mobilize members for community service: They enable many small units of individuals to pool their talents, and they often have sufficient staff to identify, plan, and organize complex activities. Without associations, the opportunities would diminish for creative service that structures new approaches or provides direct programs.

Hunger

Associations conduct a variety of community service projects that draw on their members' talents in order to meet social and economic needs. They are, for example, active in attempting to alleviate hunger; together with government programs, these private programs have been quite successful. The Grocery Manufacturers Association (GMA), Washington, D.C., for one, serves as a liaison between its members and Second Harvest, a national network of food banks, by helping to organize donations of more than 100 million pounds of food and groceries annually. This effort has multiplied Second Harvest's original distribution 40-fold. GMA also helps food banks maintain high standards of sanitation.[1]

The American Meat Institute, Arlington, Virginia, also participates in Second Harvest's network, securing well over one million pounds of meat in 1989.

The California Trucking Association (CTA), West Sacramento, participates in state food bank programs, helping to meet the large costs of transporting food. In California, food banks have spent as much as 12 percent of their budgets on transportation, with up to 20 percent of the donated food wasted because transportation was not available. CTA's program in Los Angeles coordinates the trucking routes of members' companies in order to efficiently transport donated food to food banks. Twenty-five companies participate through the association; as of last year, they had successfully transported nearly 600,000 pounds of food.

Drug and Alcohol Abuse

Associations also are involved in drug and alcohol programs, often in innovative ways. Knowing that young

"The best of association-generated community service arises from knowledge and generosity, not from guilt."

people spend a good deal of time at shopping centers, the International Council of Shopping Centers, New York, established a program to make information about drug use available in malls. In May 1987, more than 2,000 shopping centers with the help of 20,000 volunteers set up booths to support the campaign. The association estimates the attendant publicity reached 130 million people.

The American Association of Advertising Agencies (AAAA), New York, in 1987, launched a three-year "Media Advertising Partnership for a Drug-Free America." With the aim "a fundamental reshaping of social attitudes about illegal drug usage," the effort incorporates up to 50 separate campaigns, using over $500 million worth of free media time and space each year. This sum represents only part of the annual funding, however, because some agencies produce advertising at their own expense and work with other associations and corporations (Kodak, Donovan Data Systems, and the American Federation of Television Artists, for example) to create their own campaigns and monitor the results. AAAA supports the staff that guides the entire effort, under the general supervision of media, advertising, and marketing executives. Such coordination of many firms is a natural contribution of associations, whose efforts as illustrated here would be extremely hard to duplicate company by company.

The National Association of Chiefs of Police, Bethesda, Maryland, and MCI Telecommunications have for the past year conducted an extensive anti-drug effort, centering on education, prevention, and enforcement as part of a demand-reduction campaign. The association encourages school curricula that feature a no-use message based on factual information; attempts to establish drug-free school zones, showing the utility of concentrating law efforts around schools; and supports an anonymous hotline, which has led to 8,000 arrests. Efforts focusing on speakers and educational materials complete the program.

A final example of community service to fight drug use involves the activities of a national service organization. Kiwanis International, Indianapolis, mounted a far reaching public awareness campaign, using 5,500 billboards, 500 prime-time network airings of a public service announcement, a 14-week radio series, and advertising in *Time, Newsweek,* and *Sports Illustrated*. The value of the advertising alone is more than $15 million.

Literacy and Education

Associations also are active in a host of literacy and education programs. The National Society of Professional Engineers, Alexandria, Virginia, together with the National Council of Teachers of Mathematics, Reston, Virginia, CNA Insurance Companies, and the National Aeronautics and Space Administration, have developed a national program called "MATHCOUNTS." The program's goal is to turn around declining mathematical ability among American junior high school students by increasing their understanding of the importance of math, thus elevating its prestige. The program coaches students in specific curricular materials on which they then compete for awards, locally and nationally, distributes a newsletter for teachers, and sponsors teachers' workshops. More than 2 million students in 7,500 schools have participated in the program in the past seven years, and more than 30,000 schools use MATHCOUNTS material. The program is an innovative attempt to deal with a national issue by using the skills, understanding, and commitment of relevant professional associations.

The next example involves a general literacy effort by an association that is not involved in education. The 25,000-member International Association of Personnel in Employment Security (IAPES), Frankfort, Kentucky, supports a national campaign to reduce illiteracy, by providing tutors and space and educating its chapters. More than 100,000 people have been assisted through the program.

The National Association of Truck Stop Operators, Alexandria, Virginia, manages a project that uses the truck stop network to locate and identify missing children. Pictures of missing children are published in *Trucker's News*, the association's monthly magazine, and the association works with the FBI to rapidly disseminate information about missing children to drivers and other employees.

"More than 2 million students in 7,500 schools have participated in the MATHCOUNTS program."

Health Care

The Los Angeles chapter of the American Society of Interior Designers has worked to improve conditions at the Maclaren Children's Center, an emergency facility that tends to 6,000 abused, neglected, and abandoned children yearly. The chapter refurbished the center, with members designing play areas, storage facilities, observation areas, a grooming center, and general furnishings, all professionally created with the special needs of these children in mind.

The Kentucky Optometric Association, Frankfort, teamed with the American Optometric Association, St. Louis, to provide eye care to the working poor. The project has become a model for similar efforts, under the title "Vision USA." From 1985 through 1989, approximately 5,000 people have received free eye care, glasses, surgical services, and follow-up examinations.

The Medical Association of Atlanta established a clinic in 1986 in that city to provide medical care to the homeless. Since then, nearly 100 physicians have volunteered their time to help more than 2,000 people. The clinic receives donations from local hospitals and pharmacies and has steadily expanded since its inception.

American Women in Radio and Television, Washington, D.C., also is involved in a health-related project to counteract the boredom and anxiety of hospitalized children. Accordingly, the association has acquired a large library of video programs through various donations, purchased video equipment for hospitals, and worked with other organizations to develop a satellite broadcast capability.

The American Association of Neurological Surgeons, Park Ridge, Illinois, and the Congress of Neurological Surgeons, Los Angeles, established in 1986 a national head and spinal cord injury prevention program, designed to educate teenagers and young adults about the vulnerability of the head and spine and the devastation that injury can cause. The two associations produced a film discussing these realities and believe the program will reach 450,000 students this year.

Community Issues

Associations are also engaged in providing services that help to deal with public emergencies or general community problems. The Greenville Board of Realtors, South Carolina, for example, funded a fire safety house that forms the centerpiece of the city's fire safety training. The house is equipped to simulate fires, and the program developed around it teaches adults and children how to escape from a burning building. The house also was featured in a training film, and has stimulated other programs in the state.

Both the Greater Dallas Board of Realtors and the Wichita Area Board of Realtors, Kansas, organize their members once a year to paint, weatherize, and otherwise improve the homes of elderly or handicapped citizens.

The Gwinnett, Georgia chapter of the Greater Atlanta Home Builders Association has operated a program for vocational school students since 1978, in which developers donate or sell discounted lots to building trades students, who use them to construct and sell houses. The sales proceeds help finance scholarships.

The Texas Automobile Dealers Association, Austin, assisted emergency relief efforts to deal with the aftermath of a tornado that devastated Sargosa, Texas in 1987. Members donated 60 used cars and trucks to families who lost vehicles in the storm.

The Society of Louisiana Certified Public Accountants, Kenner, is donating over $1 million in professional services to help the state cope with and eventually reverse its $800 million deficit. At the governor's request, volunteers are analyzing the budget and administration of major state departments, looking for ways to eliminate or curtail programs, wasteful spending, and excessive overhead costs. Over $100 million in cuts already have been identified.

PROVIDING BROAD SUPPORT

These examples of community service organized and conducted by associations have largely centered on association efforts to fill specific needs through their members' direct expertise. There are also many association projects that strengthen or enhance the community's general functioning.

The American Bar Association (ABA), for example, is committed to a wide-ranging effort to educate Americans about the enduring importance of the U.S. Constitution, through a series of public television programs, radio and newspaper features, and conferences. Other elements include mock trials, a series of seminars, and teaching guides to help educate the young. The ABA programs have reached well over one million participants, with the aid of more than 1,000 volunteers.

State bar associations also are immersed in civic and legal education. The New York State Bar Association, Albany, for one, has worked with the state education department for the past 15 years to encourage citizenship education in public schools. More than 1,000 lawyers participate by training teachers in basic legal instruction, teaching students themselves, offering summer seminars, presenting mock trials, and providing funds to produce necessary materials.

The American Hotel and Motel Association (AHMA), and the Vote America Foundation, Washington, D.C., developed a program to help Americans vote by absentee ballot. AHMA produced and distributed a resource kit to its members, which enabled hotels to encourage absentee balloting, where appropriate, and help patrons obtain information about absentee voting in their jurisdictions.

The National Association of Broadcasters, Washington, D.C., has initiated an effort to help retrain workers displaced from declining industries. Local broadcasters attempt to band together various community resources to teach workers skills they can quickly use to seize immediate and future opportunities. Through public service announcements, NAB publicizes the training opportunities in local communities.

The Florida Independent Automobile Dealers Association, Orlando, supports battered and abused children who live in homes managed by Hope International Ministries. The association has donated a school bus, a freezer, food, cash, and the down payment and mortgage guarantee for an education and recreation building.

The Greensboro Chamber of Commerce, North Carolina, together with Lutheran Family Services, organized a project to resettle 200 Vietnamese in North Carolina homes and to help them toward economic self-sufficiency.

The Public Relations Society of America has activated its 100 chapters to develop comprehensive public relations campaigns on AIDS, illiteracy, and drug abuse.

The National Association of Life Underwriters, Washington, D.C., conducts a program of organized public service, with each of its 1,000 chapters taking responsibility for a community service project to address local issues. More than 115,000 volunteers have helped causes ranging from the Red Cross, to the Special Olympics, to the Juvenile Diabetes Foundation.

It is not necessary to belabor the social value of these community service programs. It is clear that associations organize cohesive programs that usually make direct use of their members' special skills, knowledge, and interests. In this sense, the best of associations' community service arises from knowledge and generosity, not from guilt. Many association members perform community service outside the context of their associations, and the organization that associations provide helps to increase and focus community service.

ENDNOTE

1. Many other interesting examples of community service can be found among winners of the President's Citation Program for Private Sector Initiatives. A list may be obtained from the American Society of Association Executives, Division of Public Relations, 1575 Eye St., N.W., Washington, D.C. 20005.

 # International Expertise and Technological Innovation

KEY FINDINGS

▫ One-third of the associations surveyed maintain an international affiliation.

▫ The value of associations in helping to set international standards derives from their ability "to represent technological achievement and state-of-the-art know-how."

▫ Associations can be highly influential in promoting and advancing innovative techniques that increase productivity, safety, and quality. They help enhance technological innovation by sharing practices, techniques, and advice through publications, conventions, and educational activities.

Technological innovation, grasp of international conditions, and better training for workers are and will continue to be key to America's continued economic success. For these reasons, brief discussions are warranted on associations' contributions in forming an international perspective and spurring technological innovation.

THE INTERNATIONAL MANDATE

Many associations have international members or chapters. Nearly 33 percent of the associations surveyed maintain an international affiliation, comprising 45 percent of cause-related and advocacy groups, 37 percent of professional associations, and 29 percent of trade associations. Roughly 2 percent of these associations' dues-paying members are international, and 2.5 percent of staff time is spent on international issues.

Associations can help their members achieve an international perspective in several ways. First, conventions and publications can expose members to international concerns, using common interests, professional skills, or business requirements as a springboard. These tools can help members learn about techniques that are newly invented or better developed in other countries, while affording the opportunity to sense the habits, temper, and approach of citizens of other nations.

Many learned societies participate in the international version of their associations, helping to create a set of international scholars. Medical societies have for years organized courses in other countries. Among large trade associations, international efforts are frequent. The Technical Association of the Pulp and Paper Industry, for example, publishes some of its materials in French and Spanish, and the Chemical Manufacturers Association participates in international environmental efforts.

Associations can begin to prepare their members for operating internationally. This preparation is especially important for small firms not already involved in the international arena and for businesses seeking

"The group representing the United States at international meetings is usually the same group that develops the American standard."

to explore unfamiliar markets, such as those in Eastern Europe and the Soviet Union. Some associations have operated internationally for many years, with much foreign aid and relief delivered through international nonprofits or national nonprofits with international connections.

The increasingly international economy makes international standardization and regulation particularly salient. The same forces that make standardization significant in the domestic arena also often make it significant in the international arena. It is important that international standards allow American manufacturers and service providers to produce saleable goods and that general conditions of global economic trade and growth not be stifled by excessive regulation. This nation's reliance on and bias toward voluntary, private self-regulation and quality are models for international behavior. The American National Standards Institute (ANSI), as the U.S. representative in the international standards system, is key to forwarding concerns of American business and industry.

International standardization did not grow significantly until the nongovernmental International Standards Organization (ISO) was formed in 1946. Even then, however, Americans showed little interest in harmonizing standards internationally. American export and import markets were markedly less significant than domestic markets, and U.S. standards were so widely accepted that adherence enabled U.S. products to sell in international markets. This situation began to change in the 1960s as others began to technically equal the United States, with the result that a product made according to U.S. standards often failed to meet an international standard. America's international involvement increased.

ANSI's international activities now take up one-quarter of its $8 million annual budget. It performs its international function largely through U.S. technical advisory groups, administered by trade and professional associations and sometimes government. The technical group representing the United States at international meetings is usually the same group that develops the relevant American standard. The Computer and Business Equipment Manufacturers Association, Washington, D.C., for example, is the secretariat of the committee that produces standards for American information processing and the international technical advisory group. In this way, the American group that serves as the U.S. international representative also knows most about and will be most affected by technical decisions in standard setting.

International standards are becoming so important that the theme of ANSI's 1990 public conference is, "Standardization in the 90s: Success in a Global Market." Says ANSI's president, "Standardization is particularly crucial now for international trade, as the European Community moves to create a single market by 1992."[1] The general purpose of American participation in various international regional groups that develop standards is to eliminate technical barriers to trade, barriers caused by differences in standards, as well as in laws and regulations.

Associations' role in setting international standards is central to promoting free international trade and the technological excellence that allows goods to be internationally competitive. The value of associations in helping to set international standards derives from what the president of the Standards Engineering Society, Dayton, Ohio, calls their ability "to represent technological achievement and state-of-the-art know-how." By creating standards, associations become useful forces for healthy innovation, technically and economically.

TECHNOLOGICAL INNOVATION

While setting standards can occasionally restrict innovation, more often, it facilitates concentration on quality and compatibility that focuses innovative technological efforts. Innovation also is enhanced by the sharing of practices, techniques, and advice that associations encourage through publications, conventions, and educational activities where new techniques are announced, tested, and spread.

One interesting discussion of the place of associations in encouraging innovation is found in *Professional Associations and Municipal Innovations*, a study that examined the role of associations in helping to transfer innovative techniques to city governments. The authors note that "most innovation studies at the state and local levels have suggested professional association influence." They cite a 1974 study that "examined the diffusion of technologies among state highway and air pollution control agencies and found that the relevant professional associations affected innovation adoption."[2]

The *Professional Associations and Municipal Innovation* study concentrated on associations that "have as one of their primary objectives... providing information to municipal chief executives or municipal agency line chiefs." The authors surveyed staff executives of 15 associations,

"Those associations whose information was trusted were seen as the most successful in promoting innovation."

10 composed of line managers and five serving as chief executives. According to the authors, many of these associations have "had a history of aiding municipal governments with innovations," often with federal financial support.

In addition, the authors surveyed a sample of officials from cities with populations between 25,000 and 500,000. In each case, those surveyed were to estimate "the importance, radicalness, and visibility" of the 15 innovations selected and to rank how far along they were toward adoption. Responses were analyzed, guided by a model which hypothesized that the path of innovation begins with the association staff positively evaluating the innovation and selecting a method to "transfer" the innovation, such as a workshop or publication. Other parameters evaluated included the actual transfer effort and the various decision mechanisms within the cities.

The authors concluded that staff judgments about the applicability of innovations were largely internal and individual and that staff differentiated among transfer techniques, with seminars and workshops useful in helping local managers perceive problems and publications in informing executives about effective innovations.

The effectiveness of the transfer effort was "related to certain characteristics of associations. Successful associations seem to be those with the most highly qualified staffs and the largest variety of regular transfer techniques."[3] There was, moreover, "a significant relationship between association evaluations of their success in promoting innovations and municipal officials' evaluations of that success." A significant relationship also existed between "high ratings of transfer techniques" and a city's perceptions of effective association efforts with "association success in promoting innovations."[4] Those associations whose information was trusted were seen as the most successful in promoting innovation.

The central factors in successfully adopting innovation were the city executive's ranking of its importance, attention to the transfer effort, and trust in the association's ability to influence his or her opinion about an innovation." These findings reinforce the argument that associations can be highly influential in promoting and advancing innovative techniques that increase productivity, safety, or quality.

ENDNOTES

1. American National Standards Institute, *ANSI's Role in International Standardization* (New York: ANSI, 1986).
2. Richard D. Bingham, Brett W. Hawkins, John P. Frendreis, Mary Le Blanc, *Professional Associations and Municipal Innovation* (Madison: University of Wisconsin Press, 1981), 4.
3. Ibid., 137.
4. Ibid., 138.

 # The Synergism of Associations

KEY FINDINGS

- Public benefits largely flow from the confluence of the public good and associations' educational, economic, and political needs.
- Associations have a special ability to deal with issues that cut across whole industries or professions.
- Associations through permanence and organizational structure do more overall than an ad hoc response to every problem.

"The public

benefits created

by association

activity

overshadow

instances that

fall outside

the limits."

Association codes of ethics and professional standards provide information that generally enhances consumers' trust in the reliability, quality, and safety of goods and professional services. Association performance and safety standards improve quality, reliability, and interchangeability among products and services. Association educational and research efforts improve techniques and managerial skills, add to basic knowledge, and broaden members' perspective. Associations account for nearly $50 billion in direct economic benefits and are useful in dealing with market failures. Associations are involved in significant areas of community service. Associations' activity in the political arena provides information, counters opposing views, and helps members grasp the political circumstances and conditions on which they depend.

SELF-INTEREST, RESPONSIBLY PURSUED

In all of these cases, it is the responsible collective interest of members—in advancing their knowledge, improving their products and services, increasing their skills, and enhancing their legislative standing—that brings about broader public values. While these benefits have their costs, the public value as a whole outweighs them. Indeed, it is good that it does, because associating is a constitutional right, exercised in such extraordinary variety that legislation to control particular abuses could never reform the institution were it fundamentally corrupt.

Associations are structures in which people are collectively responsible for themselves—often in a more direct and immediate way than they are through government. In this sense, associations are a school for responsible control of government. Members' collective self-interest is not identical to the whole public good, but it does serve the public in much the same way as individual self-interest does—by providing quality goods and services worth buying. That is why, for example, performance and safety standards serve both members and the public.

The pursuit of responsible self-interest requires citizens to make and honor legal and customary limits that preserve generally healthy economic and political conditions. To overstep these limits is to seek unfair advantage or, indeed, to break the law. Not hard and fast, most of these limits are set through legislation, regulation, and public opinion. The areas where associations have been questioned—actions that have restricted market access, for example—are characterized by attempts to seek unfair advantage and should be controlled. However, the many public benefits created today by responsible association activity overshadow instances that fall outside the limits.

The key point is that public benefits do not derive primarily from associations' altruism. If they did, the benefits would be fewer, for most associations are not, at center, altruistic institutions. Public benefits largely flow from the confluence of the public good and associations' own educational, economic, and political needs, responsibly pursued.

AMPLIFYING RESULTS

Although association activities bring many public benefits, one might think that other institutions also could provide these. Associations are not the only groups involved in education, for example, or even the major group. That is why each chapter has separately highlighted the special benefit associations brought about by an activity that others also perform.

Associations have a special ability to deal with issues that cut across whole industries or professions. If government is not to set all standards and codes, what institutions but associations would take the lead? Associations' activities are interconnected and often mutually supporting. Because they educate, for example, they are more likely to engage in research. Because they set and enforce codes of ethics, they are more likely to develop broad professional codes. More of each useful activity occurs because others are taking place within the same body. Associations, through their permanence and organized structure, accomplish more overall than an ad hoc response to every problem.

This interconnection among activities is visible in almost every case examined in these pages. It is also validated by observing some of the correlations among activities that emerged from the survey data.

Among trade associations, for example, expenditures form two rough clusters: (1) Forming performance and safety standards correlates significantly with activity in education, public information, and research; and (2) establishing codes of ethics and performance standards correlates significantly with education. What this means is that education and the establishment of codes of ethics and performance standards work mutually with one another, so the need for and availability of one increases the appearance of the others; and that mechanisms for public information, research, and education enhance the establishing of product and service standards.

Administrative expenditures correlate significantly with most other activities, meaning that the organized administrative activity is not merely an isolated or self-serving function but works positively with activities that have public value.

"The socially valuable activities of associations are enhanced by their overall association setting."

Within the two major clusters, the activities bear a positive relationship with one another, reinforcing the notion that associations as organizations that group activities amplify what would be accomplished were each activity pursued in a separate forum.

With professional associations, expenditures formed three basic clusters: (1) All of the information and education activities—education, public information, research, and political education—are positively associated and are also associated with community service; (2) these functions also correlate positively with setting professional standards and codes of ethics and with holding conventions; and (3) there is a strong correlation between setting and enforcing standards.

Again the connection among the various educational activities, the importance of conventions, and the relationship between education and standards point to the significance of organized associations where members meet formally and where education is important for enhancing other activities.

With cause-related and advocacy groups, information and education activities cluster among themselves, as well as with holding conventions. As with professional and trade groups, political education correlates significantly with several other association activities.

Finally, in all three types of associations, increased expenditures correlate significantly with the increased use of volunteers.

These findings are significant because they make clear that the socially valuable activities of associations are enhanced by their overall association setting. They are interrelated, not merely separate activities that come together by accident. Engaging in several activities contributes to engaging in others. It is not only that associations do several socially useful things, but that their activities are enhanced when done in association. By working for and through their members, associations produce positive synergistic effects on society.

With roots in ancient civilizations and ties to Old World guilds, associations today have evolved to occupy a unique place in America. The influence of the many nationalities constituting America's citizenry, America's geographic expanse, and, above all, the principles of her political freedom fostered independence and individualism within U.S. associations, tightly weaving them into the nation's social fabric and uniquely distinguishing them from associations of other nations.[1]

This study has identified the many ways in which this American propensity to associate benefits not only the members of any given association, but also a nation that values independence. Increasingly, associations are a vital part of American life.

ENDNOTE

1. Lee VanBremen, "The Theory of Associations," in *Attracting, Organizing, & Keeping Members*, ed. Wilford A. Butler (Washington, D.C.: American Society of Asssociation Executives, 1989), 2.